BETTER THAN EVER

DION WOODS

CREATION
HOUSE

BETTER THAN EVER: LIVE ON A LEVEL YOU NEVER THOUGHT
POSSIBLE
by Dion Woods

Published by Creation House
A Charisma Media Company
600 Rinehart Road
Lake Mary, Florida 32746
www.charismamedia.com

Better Than Ever will powerfully position you to excel in life through God's abundant grace. Dion Woods shares biblical truths that have marked his life with passion and far-reaching influence. You will be encouraged to embrace the divine influence that can and will equip you to meet your defining moment with success.

—JOHN BEVERE
AUTHOR/SPEAKER, MESSENGER INTERNATIONAL

If you're ready to go where you've never gone before, then you're ready for *Better Than Ever.*

— DR. DIMITRI BRADLEY
PASTOR, MOUNTAIN OF BLESSINGS CHRISTIAN CENTER

A clear and concise road-map to obtaining God's exceeding, abundantly above in your life.

—MARK J. WADE, MD
FOUNDER, ARISE & WALK MINISTRIES FOUNDATION

Copyright © 2011 by Dion Woods
All rights reserved

Visit the author's website: www.nextlevel-living.com

Library of Congress Control Number: 2011936188
International Standard Book Number: 978-1-61638-657-3

E-book ISBN: 978-1-61638-658-0

First edition

11 12 13 14 15 — 987654321
Printed in Canada

Editing and Concept Development by Vincent M. Newfield, New Fields & Company, P.O. Box 622, Hillsboro, Missouri, 63050. www.preparethewaytoday.org

DEDICATION

To all the people who have helped me do Better Than Ever...

My beautiful wife Belinda, for supporting, praying for and loving me for more than nineteen years.

My awesome children for reminding me daily to not sweat the little stuff.

My parents for their sacrificial love and support.

My pastors, Dr. Dimitri and Nicole Bradley for daily showing me the heart of God.

John and Lisa Bevere and the entire Messenger International Staff for your tireless and contagious passion for God.

My prayer partners, Lewis, Dawn, and Mikalya. We're going to another level.

Darren, for leading me to Christ.

Vincent, thank you for lending your incredible gift to this work and making it "better."

To my heavenly Father, for loving me beyond understanding and giving me the opportunity to represent His name in the earth.

A NOTE TO THE READER...

I am donating all of my royalties from the sales of this book to help young women and children who are victims of human trafficking. Your contribution helps in this important cause.

CONTENTS

The Lord our God said to us at Horeb, "You have stayed long enough at this mountain. Break camp and advance..."

—DEUTERONOMY 1:6–7, NIV

EXCEEDINGLY, ABUNDANTLY ABOVE

Y*OU'VE BEEN STUCK at the same place in life long enough. It's time to leave the way you've been living and pursue the life I always meant for you to live.*" This was the word God spoke to His people, the Israelites, almost three thousand years ago. But even after several millennia, it still rings prophetically true for us today. God is telling us to pursue the life He has made available for us. However, He isn't bellowing the message from the top of a mountain that rumbles with smoke and fire as He did with the Israelites. Instead, He's speaking it to the hearts of people who believe there's more to life than working a dead-end job and just paying bills.

God is calling out to those who are looking for more. He's seeking people who are desperate for purpose, desperate for change, and desperate for the kind of life that is worth living. Is that you? To those who have an ear to hear, the Spirit of God is again saying, "You've stayed long enough at this mountain. It's time to break camp and advance." And God isn't just suggesting that we do it—He's commanding us! There's a sense of urgency in His voice. It's as if we're a patient who has been wheeled into the ER on a gurney, and God is straddled over us, pounding on our chest in an effort to revive what has died on the inside of us. He's commanding us to live! "Live out the plan that I have for you," declares the Lord.

The challenge we face is how to do it. Most people want to experience everything God has for them. They want to do better. They want to reach new levels of living. However, they're unsure how to do it. We have repeatedly heard phrases like *next level* and *new level* tossed about at conferences, sporting events, and church for so long they have become more of a motivational slogan than an achievable reality. Even a search on the Internet for such terms generates almost 400 million different options. That's one for every man, woman, and child in America! Yet with all our striving to reach another level, has anyone identified a reliable path to get there? Better yet, does anyone even know what the term *next level* means?

Next-Level Concepts

God is calling out to those who are looking for more. He's seeking people who are desperate for purpose, desperate for change, and desperate for the kind of life that is worth living. Is that you?

THE BIBLE REVEALS THE ANSWER

I believe the Bible provides us with the answer to these questions in a statement the apostle Paul made to the Ephesian church. He said that God "is able to do *exceedingly abundantly above* all that we ask or think, according to the *power that works in us*" (Eph. 3:20, nkjv, emphasis added). In this statement are both the *definition* of the term *next level* and the *instructions* on how to get there. Specifically, God wants to do exceedingly, abundantly above in our lives. He wants to see us reach goals and dreams that are beyond anything we've achieved in the past. By doing so, we will have, by definition, gone to the next level. The way this occurs is by releasing the ability that God placed on the inside of us.

Let me give you an example from the sports world to illustrate what I mean. In the 2006–2007 NBA basketball season, a promising young player named Rajon Rondo was signed as a backup point guard for the Boston Celtics. During his rookie season Rondo only started in about twenty-five games but produced the following results:

- 6.4 points per game (ppg)

- 1.6 steals per game (spg)

- 3.8 assists per game (apg)

- .418 field goal percentage (ratio of non-free-throw baskets made to those attempted)

An "assist" happens when a player passes the ball to another player who then scores. Based on these results, Rondo was deemed an average NBA player during his first year. Yet on the inside of Rondo was a higher level of performance than what he had been able to release. In fact, he carried a level of ability inside of him that was *exceedingly, abundantly above* what many people thought he possessed. However, it was hidden.[1]

During Rondo's second year, something began to change. Another level of ability began to emerge. In the 2007–2008 season, Rondo went from averaging 6.4 ppg to 10.6 ppg. He also increased his assists from 3.8 apg to 5.1 apg. His field goal percentage also increased from .418 to .492.

Then in the 2008–2009 regular season, Rondo improved again. His stats were:

- 11.9 points (ppg)

- 1.9 steals per game (spg)

- 8.2 assists per game (apg)

- .505 field goal percentage

Next-Level Concepts

When you consistently produce results in your life that are exceedingly, abundantly above what you've been able to accomplish in the past, you've gone to the next level. The way you get there is by releasing the ability that's on the inside of you.

Each year, Rondo found a way to release another level of ability that God placed on the inside of him. In fact, by the end of the 2009–2010 regular season, Rondo's performance was exceedingly, abundantly above anything he had previously accomplished in the NBA. (See table below.) These results were not only unprecedented in his professional career, but they also officially placed him in a new category of exceptional performers. Everyone around the league began saying that Rondo's game had gone to the *next level*. As a result, during the 2010–2011 season, people demanded and expected much more from him.

During the 2009–2010 regular season, Rondo was producing results on the basketball court that were not only uncharacteristic of his previous NBA experience but also far beyond the skill set that many people even knew he possessed. This is what it means to go to the next level. It's when a person produces results that are exceedingly, abundantly above what they've been able to accomplish in the past. It's when they do better than ever. And it's all made possible by releasing the power God places on the inside of us.

Rajon Rondo						
Season Averages						
Season	GS	MIN	FG%	AST	STL	PTS
2006-2007	25	23.5	0.418	3.8	1.6	6.4
2007-2008	77	29.9	0.492	5.1	1.7	10.6
2008-2009	80	33	0.505	8.2	1.9	11.9
2009-2010	81	36.6	0.508	9.8	2.3	13.7

GS: Games Started	MIN: Minutes Played	FG%: Field Goal Percentage
AST: Assists	STL: Steals	PTS: Points

Source: NBA

Next-Level Concepts

Going to the next level is made possible by the power God places on the inside of you.

GOD IS ABLE

Most people have no problem with the concept that God is able to do "exceedingly, abundantly above all we can ask or think." After all, He's God! However, when you explain that He wants to do the "exceeding, abundantly above" in and through us, some people start to doubt and waver. It's as if they're waiting on God to release His power on their behalf. Meanwhile, God is waiting on them to release the power He's already given. The Bible says it is God who works in you, both to will and to do for His good pleasure (Phil. 2:13, NKJV). In other words, whatever amazing things God wants to do in the earth, He's committed to doing it through us. As crazy as it sounds, the God who can do anything has chosen to do nothing unless He does it through us. This means you could be broken in spirit, feeling empty of worth and value, and blind to the possibilities of your future, yet still become a vessel God can use to change someone's life.

This happened to me about twenty years ago during a time in my life when the presence of God seemed so far from me. I hadn't led anyone to the Lord in months, my prayer life was pretty stale, and it seemed as if God had forgotten—or worse, was purposely overlooking—me. Have you ever felt this way? Have you ever wondered if God still had a plan for your life?

These were the thoughts that sat heavy on my heart as I was flying home from a business trip one evening. I was seated next to a senior executive of a large retailer who was responsible for setting up cafes all around the world. I was tired, hungry, and a bit angry, so the last thing I wanted to do was talk. I wanted to sulk. I wanted to focus on what I felt was my insignificant role in the kingdom.

However, God had a different plan. As I took my seat, this gentleman immediately struck up a conversation. He talked about everything. He spoke about the exotic foods he ate, the places he'd been and of course, the women he met. Then came the foul language. Meanwhile, the enemy was putting thoughts in my head like, *"How is it that you get seated next to this guy? You must really be in bad shape if he can't even tell that you're a Christian."*

It only made me feel worse. Yet out of a desire to prevent the situation from going from bad to worse—and in an attempt to bring a little morality into the picture—I nudged the conversation toward God.

Amazingly, in a matter of five minutes, I found myself in full-blown witnessing mode. I was drawing diagrams, reading verses out of the Bible, and telling the guy that God had a plan for his life. Just five hours earlier, I was wondering if God had a plan for my life, and now here I was, confidently declaring

God's plan for someone I had just met. Then I asked him if I could pray for him.

That's when the heavens opened up. As I started to pray, tears started streaming down his face, and he started to sob, so much that some of the other passengers started to take notice. I couldn't believe it. God was actually using me to lead this executive to Christ! He was marvelously saved that day, and my relationship with God went to a new level. God did more than I could think or imagine that day. I'm not sure what the passengers around us were thinking while all this was going on, but I sure know what I was thinking: "God, do You want me to lead everyone on the plane to Christ?"

That was one of the greatest experiences in my life. God moved so silently yet so powerfully on that plane. He did exceedingly, abundantly above all that I could ask or think. And He can do the same for you.

I don't care how low you feel, what you've done, or what's been done to you, God can still bring you to places that seem unimaginable. Look at Oprah Winfrey. She was abused and molested as an adolescent, poor and homeless as a teen, and insecure and wounded as a young woman. Yet on the inside of her was something so big, so incredible, and so ridiculously awesome that only God could comprehend it. But once it became manifest, once she released it, Oprah was catapulted to an entirely new level of living.

Next-Level Concepts

Whatever God wants to get done in the earth realm, He's committed to doing it through us. As crazy as it sounds, the God who can do anything has chosen to do nothing unless He does it through us.

During an interview with Barbara Walters, Oprah was asked about her future plans after hosting the most successful talk show in the history of television. What could possibly be next? What was waiting for her at the next level?

Her answer gives additional insight into what it means to go to the next level. She said that she wanted to fully express everything God had placed insider of her. In other words, Oprah doesn't want to leave anything on the table. If there is something hidden within her, she wants it fully expressed to the world. In her mind, there is still more to be released.

There is also more in you. There's more that God wants to do through you—more He wants to express and more of Himself that He wants to release. It was never His intention that "exceedingly, abundantly above" be reserved only for superstar athletes or media moguls. Each of us has the ability to produce the kind of results that are truly next level. Parents can bring their parenting to new levels, kids can raise their performance in school, and we can live healthier than we previously thought or imagined. In fact, every time we utilize the power God has placed in us, we in essence let God become "able" to do the exceedingly, abundantly above in our lives. This is what it means to live at the next level.

Next-Level Concepts

Each of us has the ability to produce the kind of results that are truly next level. Every time we utilize the power God has placed in us, we in essence let God become "able" to do the exceedingly, abundantly above in our lives.

BETTER THAN EVER

When a marriage relationship goes to the next level, it will also produce results that are consistently above what the marriage has experienced in the past. If the marriage is really at the next level, then both the husband and wife will start to demonstrate love in unprecedented ways. Again, this new performance won't be temporary. In other words, the husband is not acting better just to increase his chances for sex later that night. Likewise, the wife is not doing things to ensure she gets her way in the future. They are simply responding out of a love that has been redefined and redesigned to operate better. They're listening better, speaking better, and encouraging each other better than ever before. They have committed to a new way of living. This is not to say that they don't have disagreements or that their marriage has gone from being "worse than" to "better than" all other marriages. Simply put, a marriage that has gone to the next level is one in which a couple has broken through the barrier of their own marital limitations and has established a new "high-water mark" for how they will work together in the future.

Next-Level Concepts

Next-level results are never temporary. They're
not the product of luck or chance. Instead, they
represent an entirely new standard of performance
that is both exceptional and repeatable.

The same can be said for parenting, managing your money, meeting sales goals, and even growing in your relationship with God. Realize that there is no external competition. When God brings you to the next level in any of these areas, it doesn't mean you raise your kids better, pray longer, or sell more than everyone else. It simply means that you have consistently raised your previous level of performance in these areas to such a degree that you seem unrecognizable in some way to those acquainted with your past. In other words, you're not performing like normal. You may not be better than everyone else, but you are nothing like you used to be. You're operating on what looks like a new standard, a new belief system, or a new paradigm. Simply put, you're doing better than ever.

So often we are fixated on what it takes to be the best that we forsake doing what's necessary to simply be *better*. While the notion of being the best is admirable and even enviable, the harsh reality is that, by definition, only one person can technically be the best. There's only one MVP. There's just one gold medalist for an event. Just one teacher of the year. However, everyone can be better. Everyone has the potential to perform at levels that are exceedingly, abundantly above what they can think or imagine. And wouldn't that make life much better?

Take a moment and write in the space below what your life would look like if it were better than ever. Would your spouse treat you better? Would your finances look better? Be as specific as possible. For example, you might say, "My children would live passionately for God and leave destructive relationships." How about your walk with God? What would that look like at the next level? Whatever you just imagined, you haven't even begun to scratch the surface of what God is capable and willing to do in your life!

My life would be better than ever if:

_____

_____

_____

Going to the next level means you are doing better than ever. You have consistently raised your previous level of performance in an area to such a degree that you seem unrecognizable to those acquainted with your past.

BEYOND WHAT YOU CAN THINK OR IMAGINE

When you break through to a new level of living, you can't even imagine the incredible things that will take place in your life. Literally. You can't do it. The Bible says that God's ability within in us has the capacity to produce results that are exceedingly, abundantly above all that we can *think* or *imagine!* The Amplified Version of this verse says these results are "infinitely beyond our highest prayers, desires, thoughts, hopes, or dreams" (Eph. 3:20, AMP). Now, don't get me wrong. It's not that you can't envision these things taking place. It's just that you can't imagine them happening to *you.* You can't imagine it because it's so foreign to your past experience.

For example, it's hard to imagine having enough money to pay off someone else's debt when you're drowning in your own. It's also hard to imagine having a loving relationship with your child when he's been consistently disrespectful and borderline abusive to you. Likewise, it's hard to believe that you can live pain free when your body has not functioned right for years. Yet all of these are possible when you're living better than ever.

At the next level, you will see things you have never seen before. For example, when the children of Israel entered the Promised Land, which was a type of next level for them, they saw extremely large figs and pomegranates and clusters of grapes so big that it took two men just to carry one! They

11

had never seen anything like that in Egypt. It's not that huge grapes, pomegranates, and figs never existed. The Canaanites had been enjoying them for years. It's just that they never existed at a level where the Israelites could enjoy them.

Next-Level Concepts

At the next level, you will see things
you have never seen before.

The apostle Paul also saw amazing things occur when he reached a new level of ministry. God enabled him to see things happen in his life that were so far beyond his past experience as a religious Pharisee, it was mind-blowing! According to Acts 19:12, Paul reached a place spiritually where he could simply touch a piece of clothing and the mere residue of anointing on his life would transfer to it, bringing healing to all who subsequently touched it. This was unprecedented at the level of ministry where Paul used to operate.

However, the examples I'm giving are not just limited to people in the Bible. Everyone who goes to another level will see things they've never seen before. I've experienced this in my own life. When my wife and I reached a new level of financial prosperity, we saw incredible things occur. We saw our house paid off, our cars paid for with cash, and our giving explode more than fourfold in a single year. We saw things happen in our finances that were literally unprecedented. We were able to not only put our children into private school but also pay for others to attend. We literally went from renting a one-bedroom apartment to owning three homes! Trust me, after living as a renter for seven years, it was hard to imagine myself being an owner, even though the capacity to be an owner lived inside me. Yet once I began to release the ability

God had given me, I began to live on a whole new level—and the same level of living is available to you!

LEVELS OPERATE BY LAWS

Unfortunately, life at the level that I'm talking about doesn't manifest itself just because you desire it. Wouldn't that be nice? Instead, new levels of living are achieved when people cooperate with specific laws that govern the release of God's power within them. However, in order to benefit from these laws, it's important to understand the purpose of laws and why they exist.

A law is an irrefutable truth that governs how something works. For example, the law of gravity governs how objects with mass are attracted to each other. Without gravity, planets would drift randomly into space—or worse, collide into one another. The law of gravity prevents this from happening. Furthermore, this law is irrefutable in that it cannot be changed, altered, or denied, except by the introduction of a higher-order law. By this I mean that the law of gravity will affect everything and everyone that comes in contact with it, unless you engage a higher-order law that will override it.

Unfortunately, some laws work against us. For example, the Bible says that mankind was held captive by sin for thousands of years because of the law of sin and death. This law was activated in the earth by the actions of the first man created, Adam. Scripture explains:

> *Therefore, as sin came into the world through one man [Adam], and death as the result of sin, so death spread to all men, [no one being able to stop it or to escape its power] because all men sinned.*
> —ROMANS 5:12, AMP, EMPHASIS ADDED

Notice that the power of sin and its consequence of death was a force no one could escape. It affected everything and everyone. It couldn't be changed, altered, or denied. It was irrefutable. This is why the apostle Paul called it a law:

> *For in my inner being I delight in God's law; but I see another law at work in me, waging war against the law of my mind and making me a prisoner of the law of sin at work within me.*
>
> —ROMANS 7:22–23, EMPHASIS ADDED

Next Level Concepts

A law is an irrefutable truth that cannot be changed or denied except by a higher-order law. It is irrefutable.

Through his sin, Adam caused everyone born after him to become imprisoned by the law of sin and death. As a result, all of mankind was subject to committing selfish acts that at times seemed beyond their ability to control. They wanted to do right, but they were incapable of performing it. They wanted to live above the cravings of the flesh, but they kept finding themselves stuck in the very things they hated. Paul sums up living under the law of sin and death well, saying:

> *I realize that I don't have what it takes. I can will it, but I can't do it. I decide to do good, but I don't really do it; I decide not to do bad, but then I do it anyway. My decisions, such as they are, don't result in actions. Something has gone wrong deep within me and gets the better of me every time.*
>
> —ROMANS 7:18–20, THE MESSAGE

Paul describes the law of sin and death as being born with a genetic disposition toward living in opposition to God's will. No wonder he cried out, "Who will rescue me from this body that is subject to death?" (Rom. 7:24). Under this law, man's relationship with God was cut off. And the law couldn't be changed or denied. It was irrefutable.

But thank God for a higher-order law! In His infinite mercy, He introduced us to a higher-order law that nullified the effects of the law of sin and death—that is, the law of the Spirit of life in Christ Jesus. The apostle Paul describes the freedom of this law saying:

> *There is therefore now no condemnation to those who are in Christ Jesus, who do not walk according to the flesh, but according to the Spirit. For the law of the Spirit of life in Christ Jesus has made me free from the law of sin and death.*
> —ROMANS 8:1–2, NKJV, EMPHASIS ADDED

Again, thank God for His higher-order law! Those who live by the law of the Spirit of life in Christ Jesus can live free from the law of sin and death. We do this by walking in the strength of God's grace, thus nullifying the deeds of our flesh. Like the aviators of old, we don't have to remain bound to the ground. The sky is the limit! Yet if we're unfamiliar with the law of the Spirit of life in Christ Jesus—or worse, unwilling to live by it—we will remain subject to the law of sin and death—a life God never intended for us to live.

Let's go back to the law of gravity for a moment to bring closure to this point. For thousands of years the law of gravity kept men limited to the ground. This was not because they didn't want to fly but because they didn't understand the laws that made flight possible. However, once men began to understand and engage higher-order laws, such as the three laws of motion, it enabled them to do what they could never do before: fly. Think about it. One law restricted us to the ground. Another law allowed us to fly like a bird. What we experienced depended on what law we put in motion.

Next-Level Concepts

Like the aviators of old, we don't have to remain bound to the ground. The sky is the limit! As we live by the law of the Spirit of life in Christ Jesus, we can live free from the law of sin and death.

I believe the same truth applies to reaching goals and dreams that seem impossible. There are laws that govern the release of God's "exceedingly, abundantly above" in our lives. I call them the laws of the next level. And like all laws, they are irrefutable, in that they cannot be changed or denied except by the introduction of higher-order laws. Cooperate with these laws, and you will go to places you never dreamed possible. Violate them, and you will forever struggle trying to reach the place God has ordained for you. In the next chapter, I want to eliminate the struggle and show you how to go where you've never gone before.

TO ENTER A NEW LEVEL, YOU CAN'T BE CONTENT WITH YOUR CURRENT LEVEL

*C*ONTENTMENT. IT'S SUCH a gentle and peaceful word. Whenever I hear it, I envision a small baby lamb safely nestled in the arms of Jesus. It sounds so comforting. Yet in reality, contentment can be harmful, even deadly, to those who are trying to do better.

Of course, such statements go against the grain of most religious teaching. It's true that the Bible commands us to be content. The apostle Paul made this clear when he said godliness with contentment is great gain and that we should keep our lives free from the love of money and be content with what we have (1 Tim. 6:6; Heb. 13:5). In saying this, he means that we should be content where God tells us to be content. However, we should not be satisfied to live on a level with which God is not satisfied.

So the question of contentment needs to be asked in a different context. Specifically, is God content for us to stay where we currently are in our lives, or is He looking for us to do something more? Is He satisfied with what we are producing, or is He expecting another level of His power to be released in and through us? I believe He's looking for more. I believe there is more destiny, more victory, and more purpose to be fulfilled. There's more love to show, more lives to save, more money to give, and more discoveries to be made. In fact, the only time God will stop looking for more fruit from our lives is when we leave the planet. Until then, He's looking for more. If He wasn't, then He would have never made the following statement:

> *I am the true grapevine, and my Father is the gardener. He cuts off every branch of mine that doesn't produce fruit, and he prunes the branches that do bear fruit so they will produce even more.*
> —JOHN 15:1–2, NLT, EMPHASIS ADDED

Notice the gardener in this story is not content with the fruit the branches are bearing. He's thankful for the fruit but not content with the amount. The gardener knows that the branches have the ability to produce even more. So what does he do? He prunes them to get another level of fruit bearing. Keep in mind whom Jesus identifies as the gardener: our heavenly Father. We are the branches He is talking about. This means you can almost read this same verse as follows: "God the Father is the Gardener. We are the branches. Every person who claims to have God as His Father but doesn't bear fruit will be judged. And even the people who are producing results that God always intended will be encouraged to produce even more."

Hence, I don't believe God is content for us to live beneath the level of ability He's placed inside of us. To do so would be a waste of His rich treasure. This is why contentment can be an enemy to us as we seek the next level. It's an enemy because it disguises waste as gratefulness. That is, it suggests that by seeking more in life, we are ungrateful in some way for what we've been given. However, that's not how God views it.

Next-Level Concepts

Is God content to keep you where you currently are in life, or is He looking for you to do something more? Is He satisfied with what you are producing, or is He expecting another level of His power to be released in and through you?

As the Old Testament judge Jephthah stated so well, "Whatever the LORD our God has given us, we will possess" (Judg. 11:24). In other words, if God still has something available for us, we should not be satisfied until we possess it. This is where discontentment is healthy. People who go from one level to the next do so because they don't believe it's the will of God for them to stay where they are. In fact, they almost hate staying at their current level. Now, I'm not talking about being ungrateful or spoiled, nor am I talking about hatred that consumes people with bitterness and rage. On the contrary, the type of "hate" I'm talking about is what the dictionary describes as "a feeling of dislike so strong that it demands action." It's an unrelenting cry that simply says, "Something's gotta change, and it's gotta change soon."

A POWERFUL LESSON FROM FOUR LEPERS

The Bible gives us a great example of how discontentment can be a healthy motivation for change. In 2 Kings 7, there is a story of four lepers who were forced to sit outside the gate of Samaria during a time of war. As lepers, religious law forbade them from entering the city to prevent others from becoming infected with their disease. However, at this particular time there was a war taking place, and they were caught right in the middle of it. On one side was a walled city that refused to let them in. On the other was an invading army that had no problem killing anyone who got in their way.

Next-Level Concepts

> If God still has something available for you,
> you should not be satisfied until you possess
> it. People who go from one level to the next
> do so because they don't believe it's the will
> of God for them to stay where they are.

So there they sat, stuck between the proverbial rock and a hard place. The Bible doesn't say how long they stayed at that level of existence. It could have been hours or days or even weeks. I'm sure they wanted a better life than the one they were seemingly dealt, but they didn't see any way to get it. They were stuck. Where could they go? Who would accept them? And so they sat...and sat. They hoped things would change, but they didn't. They prayed for someone to come and make their lives better, but no one came. They sat there until they grew tired of sitting and waiting. Then, suddenly, something began to change—not on the outside, but on the inside of them. The moment their discontent reached a tipping point, they asked themselves a very important question:

Why stay here?

—2 Kings 7:3

"Why stay here?" It's the question every person who seeks a higher level must ask himself or herself before they can escape their present level. *Why stay* with the same unhealthy lifestyle when we desire to look and feel better? *Why stay* in unforgiveness and bitterness when what we really want is to be at peace and free of anger and strife? *Why settle* for a weekly paycheck when what we really want is an equity stake in the business? Until we run out of answers to the question "Why?" we will stay stuck at our present level.

The lepers ran out of answers. They couldn't justify staying another day in their present condition. So they broke camp and advanced. Notice that their discontentment fueled their action. As long as they tolerated the life they were living, they had no motivation to seek something better. But once they could tolerate their conditions no longer, motivation for a better life gave birth to change.

Next-Level Concepts

"Why stay here?" It's the question every person who seeks a higher level must ask himself or herself before they can escape their present level.

WHY STAY IN SOMETHING THAT DOESN'T PRODUCE LIFE?

Let me give you a personal example of how discontentment can be a force for good in your life. Several years ago my wife and I purchased a home in the state of Virginia. It was a blessing from God and by far our largest investment. However, the debt we incurred to buy the home really bothered me. We could afford the house, but I struggled with the fact that we would end up paying hundreds of thousands of dollars in interest over the next thirty years. I hated the thought of being in debt for three decades! Yes, I was grateful for what God had given us. However, I wasn't content to relish in a lifestyle of debt. I kept asking myself, "Why live with it?"

The Bible says in Romans 13:8 to owe no man anything but to love him. So it was clear to me that something had to change. It was only after I became fed up with our debt that I became empowered to try and free myself of it. Accordingly, we made immediate changes that were simple, yet profound. Instead of using the extra money we earned each month to buy more things, we used it to pay down our mortgage. Rather than buying a new car, we bought a used one. Instead of furnishing every room, we put the extra cash down on principal. Month after month, quarter after quarter, and year after year, we effectively paid down the principal on our mortgage loan.

Now, don't get me wrong. When we first started doing this, it didn't seem like anything was happening. However, in time we started to notice a change. Slowly our principal balance started to decline. Finally, we were making progress. Then something else happened. I began gaining new clients on my job. I started winning new business and receiving larger and larger commission checks. Coincidence? I doubt it. It seemed like the moment we became serious about getting out of debt, the power to do so showed up. In the end, we literally saved over $300,000 in interest and paid off the house in less than six years!

Next-Level Concepts

The Bible says in Romans 13:8 to owe no man anything but to love him. It is only after we become fed up with debt that we become empowered to free ourselves of it.

Several of my friends have done the same thing. One couple we know paid off their home in less than ten years while earning under $150,000 a year. This is pretty phenomenal when you consider that the government gets about 30 percent of their income in taxes each year. They also did it while raising four children, giving faithfully to their church, and contributing to a 401k plan. In the natural realm, this seems impossible. And actually, it is. Yet somehow God was able to do exceedingly, abundantly above all they could ask or think.

I firmly believe that the discontentment with debt was key

here. In other words, our friends hated living in debt so much that they were willing to make changes in their lifestyle to be free of it. If this meant refinancing their mortgage from thirty to fifteen years, they were willing to do it. If it meant forgoing short-term pleasures in order to make extra payments on their house, they were willing to do it. If it meant postponing the purchase of a new car in order to pay down debt, they were willing to do it. They prayed for ways to earn extra money, and God showed them how.

It was only when these friends stood in agreement and demonstrated to God that they were serious about changing their current level that the power to perform it showed up. Suddenly, bonuses began to appear at work. New clients started signing up. Windows of opportunity began to open. Was it a coincidence? Again, I think not! They simply employed a law. They realized that if they wanted to live at a new level called "debt free," they would first have to hate living at a level called "debt-ridden."

NEW LEVELS OF FREEDOM
FROM ADDICTION

This law of not being content with your current level doesn't just empower you to eliminate mortgages or pay off credit cards. It can also reverse failing grades in school, free you from domestic abuse, help you lose weight, and even break addictions off your life.

My mother is living proof of this truth. She was a heavy smoker for more than thirty years, and I hated it. When I turned eighteen, she would make me go to the local convenience store about once a week to buy her a new pack of cigarettes. It's not that she didn't understand what the cigarettes were doing to her. It's just that the law of addiction refused to let her be free of them. Like many smokers, she attempted to stop several times, but to no avail. The situation seemed hopeless.

On one occasion she even went up for prayer at her local church to be delivered from smoking. However, when her pastor asked her for the cigarettes in her purse she refused to let go of them. She was ready for freedom but she wasn't ready for the change that freedom required.

However, about fifteen years ago, something happened. My mom was asked by the pastor to serve in a semi-leadership capacity. While thrilled with the opportunity, she felt an immediate internal conflict. "How can I be an example to others in the church when I'm still so controlled by cigarettes?" she thought. For weeks she struggled within. She desperately wanted to get more involved in the things of God, but in her mind the cigarettes were holding her back.

More and more, her hatred for the habit grew. She hated that she had to hide when she smoked, and she hated feeling like a hypocrite. Then one day, her level of discontentment finally rose to such an extent that it prompted her to take action.

Now, remember, she wanted to stop smoking for years. She disliked it—for years! However, the power to actually stop didn't show up until she ran out of answers to the question, *Why wait?*

That Sunday, when the pastor asked for people who wanted prayer to come forward, my mom did (again!). She had finally made up her mind that enough was enough. She was going to move forward and take hold of the new things God had for her, and nothing—not even cigarettes—was going to stop her. She hasn't smoked since! The power to break free from what once held her didn't show up in her life until she refused to stay in a place that God had abandoned. If God did it for her, He can do it for you!

Make up your mind that enough is enough.
Decide to move forward and take hold of
the new things God has for you. Don't let
anything, including addictions, stop you.

DON'T SETTLE FOR LESS THAN GOD'S BEST!

Whenever you settle for your current level, you close the door on the next level by default. The word *settle* means "to become fixed or take up residence." When we settle, we take up residence in a place that God never intended for us to remain. This is what happened to a man in the Bible named Terah. Terah was the father of the patriarch Abraham (or Abram), the man God selected to establish a special covenant. Listen to the account of his calling:

> *The Lord had said to Abram, "Leave your native country, your relatives, and your father's family, and go to the land [Canaan] that I will show you. I will make you into a great nation. I will bless you and make you famous, and you will be a blessing to others. I will bless those who bless you and curse those who treat you with contempt. All the families on earth will be blessed through you."*
> —GENESIS 12:1–3, NLT, EMPHASIS ADDED

In Genesis 12, we learn that God told Abraham to leave his family and go the land of Canaan. Yet upon closer examination of Scripture, we see that Abraham's father, Terah, attempted to make the same journey to Canaan with his family many years earlier. This is found in the last few verses of chapter 11:

> *Terah took his son Abram, his grandson Lot son of
> Haran, and his daughter-in-law Sarai, the wife of
> his son Abram, and together they set out from Ur of
> the Chaldeans to go to Canaan.*
> —GENESIS 11:31, EMPHASIS ADDED

Notice that Terah began his journey to Canaan long before Abraham was instructed to go. Could it be that the call of God was *first* given to Terah? Could it be that God only chose Abraham after his father refused to fully obey? The Bible doesn't say. However, we do know that Terah had every intention of going to Canaan. Unfortunately, something prevented him from getting there. The verse continues:

> *But when they came to Haran, they settled there.*
> —GENESIS 11:31, EMPHASIS ADDED

Isn't it crazy how you can intend to do one thing with your life but settle for something else? You intended to get your college degree but settled for a job that put some money in your pocket. You intended to marry someone who shared your values and beliefs but settled for someone you hoped would change. You intended to exercise four days a week but settled for just one day because your schedule was too busy.

That is what Terah did—he settled. He wanted and intended to go to Canaan, but he settled for Haran. The really sad part is what happened after he settled:

> *Terah lived 205 years, and he died in Haran.*
> —GENESIS 11:32, EMPHASIS ADDED

Terah died in the thing he settled for. He wanted Canaan but settled for Haran, and that's where he died. This is why you and I can't settle or be content to live in anything less than God's best. Where we settle is where we live. Furthermore, our choices affect not only us but also our children and our children's children. For example, I know of families who lived in the same inner-city projects for generations. The grandmother lived in the projects. So did her daughter. And then the granddaughter. For some reason, they couldn't break the cycle. They couldn't break free.

The same can be said for education. There are families that have never had anyone attend or graduate from college. However, inevitably, one day a child is born who breaks the cycle. The parent who never attended college gets to the point where he refuses to see his child follow the same pattern. And that's when the power to do exceedingly, abundantly above shows up. Discontentment reaches a boiling point, and a refusal to accept the status quo emerges. Suddenly, the thing that once held a family in bondage is broken, and a child is able to do what no one else in her family has done.

Next-Level Concepts

Whenever you settle for your current level, you close the door on the next level by default. Don't settle or be content to live in anything less than God's best.

So let's apply this same principle to your life. What are you trying to achieve? Where are you trying to go? What new level are you trying to reach? Until your level of discontentment rises to a point where you refuse to stay where you are, you will never experience the level you desire. At some point you have to look in the mirror and ask yourself one simple question: **Why settle for less?**

WAKE UP AND SMELL THE COFFEE

Thankfully, it doesn't require a PhD to recognize when you are settling. In general, there are six ways to recognize when you're settling for less than God's best in your life:

> ### *"How to Know When You're Settling"*
>
> *1. You're willing to accept less, even though your heart is crying for more*
>
> *2. You no longer have the energy or desire to do what's required to reach your dreams and goals.*
>
> *3. Your actions become defined by your excuses instead of your passion*
>
> *4. You talk more about your past than your future*
>
> *5. You see someone else living out your dream, but it no longer moves you*
>
> *6. You no longer believe it's possible to do better*

You'll know you are settling when you choose to accept something your heart has rejected. In other words, there will be a longing in your soul for something more satisfying and enduring than what you're currently experiencing.

This is what happened with Howard Schultz, CEO of Starbucks Coffee. By the age of twenty-eight, he was comfortably positioned in a company that sold kitchen equipment and housewares. He was earning almost $200,000 a year (in today's dollars), had a company car, an expense account, and free trips to Sweden several times a year. What a life! Yet after three years of living at this level, something began to stir on the inside of Howard. His heart began to cry for more. Here's the way he described it in his book *Pour Your Heart Into It:*

> *The life I was leading was beyond my parents' best dreams for me. Most people would be satisfied with it. So no one—especially my parents—could understand why I was getting antsy. But I sensed*

that something was missing. I wanted to be in charge of my own destiny. It may be a weakness in me: I'm always wondering what I'll do next. Enough is never enough.[2]

Enough is never enough? This guy sounds like the gardener in the parable Jesus told. What more could he possibly want? He had a company car, free air travel to incredible destinations, and a great salary. Yet he realized that if he wanted to go to the next level, he couldn't be content to stay where he was. He had to reach for something more.

Unfortunately, some viewed his actions as excessive or perhaps greedy. "There he is with more money and power than most people could wish for," they whined. "And he's saying 'enough is not enough'?" But greed wasn't motivating Mr. Schultz. The desire for the next level was. Money wasn't calling him. A lifetime opportunity with Starbucks was. That was the reason he refused to settle at his current level. His heart was crying out for more, and he would not be denied. How many of us can say the same?

In Scripture, Terah settled for Haran when his heart was crying for Canaan. Abraham's wife settled for Ishmael when her heart was crying for Isaac. The children of Israel settled for the "leeks and onions" of Egypt when their hearts were crying for the "milk and honey" of the Promised Land. When we know in our heart that God has more for our life, we can't allow ourselves to settle for anything less.

So ask yourself a question. Have you given up on a dream and settled for something less? Does it fulfill the longing in your heart? The answer for most of us is no. Settling never satisfies; it only briefly quiets the voice of a heart that's crying out for something more. It's only when you respond to that cry that real change begins to emerge in your life.

Next-Level Concepts

Never settle for something less when your heart is crying for more. Settling never satisfies. It only briefly quiets the voice of a heart that's crying out for more.

HUNGER IS A POWERFUL MOTIVATOR

Returning to the story of the lepers, we discover that discontentment with their current level wasn't the only thing that prompted them to leave what had become familiar. Hunger was also a driving force. Listen again to what they said:

> *Why should we sit here, waiting to die? There's nothing to eat in the city, so we would starve if we went inside. But if we stay out here, we will die for sure. Let's sneak over to the Syrian army camp and surrender. They might kill us, but they might not.*
>
> —2 KINGS 7:3–4, CEV

The lepers had come to a point where the craving for a better life was too great to ignore. Hunger will do that to you—it will make you seek the thing you crave. This is why Jesus said, "Blessed are those who hunger and thirst for righteousness, for they will be filled" (Matt. 5:6). Hunger is a signal that something is deficient and needs to change. Without hunger, there's no real incentive to search for that which satisfies.

This principle was illustrated well in Dr. Spence Johnson's best-selling book *Who Moved My Cheese?*[3] In it he tells an animated story of two sets of mice who journey through a maze to find cheese. They are Sniff and Scurry and Hem and Haw. One day the group stumbles upon a large pile of cheese in a place called Cheese Station C. Once they find the cheese, Hem and Haw immediately announce their retirement from the cheese-hunting business. They take off their shoes and declare an official end to hunger. "No more waking up early and walking down endless corridors to find cheese!" they cheered. In other words, "Why search for the next level of cheese when we're satisfied with the level we currently possess?"

Companies that have relied on such logic have failed. So have some individuals' careers. This erroneous line of thinking believes, "Why change or improve our occupational skills when the ones we possess are putting food on the table?" Unfortunately, this type of thinking has also infiltrated many churches. In this case, leaders falsely think, "Why institute new programs and services in the ministry when the ones we have are meeting the needs?" Some individuals have also taken on this kind of mind-set when it comes to their health. They think, "Why improve my diet when my weight and health seem just fine? If things are OK, let them be. Why raise the bar?"

Next-Level Concepts

Hunger is a powerful, driving force. It's a signal that something is deficient and needs to change. Without hunger, there's no real incentive to search for that which satisfies.

This was the mind-set of Hem and Haw. Needless to say, after several days of eating buckets of cheese, their hunger left. Unfortunately, they didn't realize that when they lost their hunger, they lost something much more important to their future success. They lost their ability to improve. The other mice in the story, Sniff and Scurry, responded differently. They never let their stomachs become full at the expense of their souls. They remained hungry. So when the cheese ran out in Cheese Station C, Sniff and Scurry quickly began hunting for more cheese. Hem and Haw, however, couldn't accept the truth. They just couldn't believe the cheese was gone. Day after day, they came back to the same empty place, hoping that somehow a new pile of cheese had reappeared. But it never did.

Like the lepers described in the Bible, days went by until Hem and Haw finally grew tired of living in lack. A strong dislike for their current level of living slowly arose in their hearts, and a desire for change emerged. Fueled by this new passion, they laced up their shoes and began to search for something better. Hunger had finally set in.

CHANGE WILL COME BY REVELATION OR REVOLUTION

The characters described in *Who Moved My Cheese?* validate a simple truth: people are either internally driven to change or externally compelled to change. I call it change by *revelation* or change by *revolution*.

Without question, change is inevitable. But how it comes and the type of effects it brings are greatly up to us.

Change by *revelation* occurs when you internally decide to act before a situation demands it of you. Steve Jobs, CEO of Apple Computer, echoed this truth when he spoke to the Stanford University graduating class of 2005. He said:

> For the past thirty-three years, I have looked in the mirror every morning and asked myself: "If today were the last day of my life, would I want to do what I am about to do today?" And whenever the answer has been "No" for too many days in a row, I know I need to change something.[4]

Change by *revolution*, on the other hand, occurs when external forces and circumstances compel you to change before you're ready to do so. This could be a doctor telling you that you have heart disease, your company telling you they have downsized and eliminated your position, or your spouse telling you he or she wants a divorce. Change by revolution always seems sudden, cruel, and costly. It feels this way because you're not prepared to receive it. And change is always best received by those who are prepared for it.

Next-Level Concepts

Change by *revelation* occurs when you internally decide to act before the situation demands it of you. Change by *revolution* occurs when external circumstances compel you to change before you're ready. Change is best received by those prepared for it.

WHAT HAPPENED TO THE LEPERS?

So, what happened to the lepers? Well, the Bible says they refused to sit around and wait until their circumstances changed. Instead, they changed:

> *So at twilight they set out for the camp of the Arameans. But when they came to the edge of the camp, no one was there! For the Lord had caused the Aramean army to hear the clatter of speeding chariots and the galloping of horses and the sounds of a great army approaching. "The king of Israel has hired the Hittites and Egyptians to attack us!" they cried to one another. So they panicked and ran into the night, abandoning their tents, horses, donkeys, and everything else, as they fled for their lives. When the lepers arrived at the edge of the camp, they went into one tent after another, eating*

and drinking wine; and they carried off silver and gold and clothing and hid it.

—2 Kings 7:5–8, nlt

Notice what happened when the lepers made a change. In as little as a few hours, they went from being hungry to being full. They went from poverty to wealth—from sadness to joy! They had made the leap from one level of living to the next.

But what triggered it? What made the difference? Why did God wait so long to do such an amazing miracle? I believe the answer is that He could have done it days or weeks earlier. However, these men were bound by a law that could not be altered: *to reach the next level, you can't be content with your current level.* However, the moment they changed what they were willing to tolerate, breakthrough occurred.

Amazingly, the story doesn't end there. After the lepers made their life-changing discovery, they decided to go back to the very city that rejected them and share the good news about what had happened in the Syrian camp. As a result, the entire city was rescued. Listen to the account:

At once the people [in the city] went to the Syrian camp and carried off what was left. They took so much that a large sack of flour and two large sacks of barley sold for almost nothing, just as the Lord had promised.

—2 Kings 7:16, cev, emphasis added

Here's my point. You never know how a change in your life will affect a change in someone else's life. I'm sure the lepers had no idea that a simple decision to leave what was familiar and pursue what God was making available could affect so many people. Their choice moved an entire city from a place of poverty and lack to a place of "exceedingly, abundantly above."

So what should this say to you? I believe it says that there's more on the line than just your future. Your children need you to go to the next level. Your coworkers need you to go to the next level. Even your nation needs you to go to the next level. There are God-breathed answers to problems that plague others on the inside of you. Yet as long as you remain content to live beneath the level God is calling you to live, you aren't just hindering yourself but also those who can't get to their place of destiny without you. Believe it or not, there is someone out there right now whose breakthrough might hinge upon how long you continue to dwell at your mountain. Like God, they need you to not only break camp but also to advance to your next level.

Next-Level Concepts

You never know how a change in your life will affect someone else. There are God-breathed answers to problems that plague others on the inside of you. Don't be content with your current level. Break camp and advance to the next.

NEXT-LEVEL ACTION STEPS

1. Describe an area in your life that you'd like to see elevated to the next level.

_____

_____

_____

2. What do you think is holding you back from reaching it?

_____

_____

_____

3. Have you settled for something less than God's best? If so, what is it?

_____

_____

_____

4. What changes and/or sacrifices are you willing to make in order to get there?

_____

_____

_____

Activity for Advancement: Take a blank sheet of paper and draw a line down the center of it. On the left, describe your life as it exists today. Include your finances, your family, and your friends. Describe your health, your job, and your relationship with God. On the right side, describe how your life would look at the next level. When you're finished, take the paper to God in prayer. Ask Him for direction and the strength and discipline you need to carry out what He shows you.

Scriptures for Meditation: Psalm 25; 32:8; Isaiah 30:21; James 1:5

IT TAKES MORE POWER TO BREAK OUT OF A LEVEL THAN IT DOES TO STAY IN IT

IT'S 2:25 A.M. on March 11, 2008, and the astronauts aboard the space shuttle *Endeavor* are about to take the ride of their lives. In a matter of moments, millions of pounds of ammonium propellant will be ignited under their seats, blasting them twenty-eight miles into the air in less time than it takes to eat an order of french fries at McDonald's. What's amazing about their journey is not the speed at which they will travel, which is 17,500 miles per hour. It's the power required to lift them from one level of existence to the next. Not only must their spacecraft overcome its own weight of 4.5 million pounds, but it must also overcome the restraining force of gravity that attempts to pull it back to the earth. In other words, if the *Endeavor* hopes to break free to another level in space, it must produce more power than the force of gravity holding it on the ground.

The same applies in our lives. It takes more power to break free from a level than it does to stay in it. Take weight loss as an example. Getting rid of the first five to seven pounds of excess weight is relatively easy if you stick with an effective diet and exercise program. However, getting rid of the next ten pounds is another story. In order to lose the next ten, you often have to increase the intensity and/or method of your training. Fitness trainers call this breaking through a plateau.

I faced a different type of plateau when I went from renting to owning a home. My wife and I spent seven years as renters before we amassed the level of financial power needed to break through to home ownership. I remember walking in neighborhoods for years, looking at homes and wondering if I would ever experience a breakthrough. What it took for me to remain a renter was clearly not enough for me to become an owner. I would need more.

Let me give another example to illustrate this law. This time, let's look at churches. According to a 2009 National Congregations Study,[5] the average congregation has about seventy-five regular participants. However, most people prefer to attend a church that has at least four hundred members. So if your church is small (seventy-five to one hundred members), then the challenge is breaking through to next level (four hundred members). But how do you do it? Some churches have spent years trying to break through to the four-hundred-member level. Clearly the power needed to maintain and serve seventy-five members is different from the power needed to attract, retain, and serve four hundred members. Usually it takes a new release of God's power that exceeds what the church has experienced in the past. That's when the membership goes to from one hundred to four hundred.

In order to go from four hundred to one thousand members, a breakthrough must occur again. There must be a new release of power—power that exceeds what the congregation has experienced in the past. Perhaps the love has to increase, the outreach improve, or the message become more relevant. Perhaps the structure of the services need to change or the worship become more authentic. Maybe the leaders' commitment to prayer needs to improve or the fear of the Lord needs to saturate the house in a fresh way. It varies by church, but one thing is consistent: *it takes greater power to break out of a level than it does to stay in it.* When this power shows up, nothing can hold you back.

Unfortunately, the thing that holds us isn't always what we

imagine. Sometimes our greatest fight is not against external forces but against our own harmful habits and mind-sets. Like the space shuttle *Endeavor*, our challenge isn't just breaking free to go to another level. It's getting rid of harmful weights that are weighing us down, like the weight of poor thinking.

Next-Level Concepts

If we want to break free to go to higher levels of living, we not only need to know what's holding us back. We also need enough power to break free from it.

THE WEIGHT OF POOR THINKING

The weight the space shuttle *Endeavor* carries is enormous. Similarly, the faulty mind-sets and beliefs that people often carry through life are just as significant. This is why the Bible instructs us to "strip off every weight that slows us down, especially the sin that so easily trips us up" (Hcb. 12:1, NLT). We can desire to go to the next level of living, but if we are carrying excess baggage, the journey will be more difficult, if not impossible, to take. We can work hard with all our might but still struggle under the weight of what I call "hidden cargo." I believe the weight of poor thinking is the most significant of these.

In simple terms, poor thinking is a mind-set that causes you to believe and focus on something that is untrue and destructive to the future God has for you. It's literally the opposite of what God thinks about you. For example, you can think you are unattractive, but God thinks you're beautiful (Ps. 139:14). You can think you are unqualified to do something, but God thinks you are able to do anything He asks you to do by His strength (Phil. 4:13). You can think you're a loser, but God says you are a winner—you are more than a conqueror through Him (Rom. 8:37).

If you've ever spent time meditating on financial problems, worrying about your children, or fretting over a medical condition, then you have probably run up against poor thinking. These thoughts sound like, "I'm too old." "Nothing ever works out for me." "Why even try?" "I'll never get better." Such thinking will always hold us back from the future God has planned for us. It must be identified and disposed of.

Next-Level Concepts

Poor thinking is a mind-set that causes you to believe and focus on something that is untrue and destructive to the future God has for you.

Unfortunately, it's all too easy to see other people as the thing holding us back. We have thoughts like, "If only my boss wasn't such a jerk, I would have received that promotion." Or, "If my husband was more supportive, I would be further along in life." Or, "If they weren't racist, I would have received the job." And on and on the list goes. These statements may have merit. People can and do affect our journey to the next level. However, the weight of their impact is minimal in comparison to the damage of receiving and meditating on poor thinking and faulty beliefs.

Consider the Israelites' journey to the Promised Land. When ten of the twelve spies who were sent to search out the land returned and were interviewed by Moses, they gave the following reasons they could not possess their next level of living:

- "The people who live there are powerful."

- "The cities are fortified and very large."

- "We saw giants in the land."

- "The land we explored devours those living in it."

- "We seemed like grasshoppers in our own eyes."
  (See Numbers 13:26–33.)

Sadly, the majority of the Israelites believed this report that was filled with poor thinking. In their eyes, external circumstances and people were the problem. They wanted to live at another level, but they thought other people had the power to stop them from walking in it. They wanted a better life, but they believed unforeseen circumstances were denying them the opportunity to experience it. Again, in their eyes, they weren't the problem. Everybody and everything else was!

When God gave His assessment of the situation to Moses, He had a very different take on why Israel couldn't advance. According to Him, they were not able to enter the Promised Land because of their unbelief. (See Hebrews 3:19.) In other words, Israel's poor thinking had a much greater impact on their future than any Canaanite army ever could. The Israelites' thoughts were wrong. They believed they weren't capable of conquering the land. Consequently, they could only perform to the level of their thinking. Since they couldn't think well, they couldn't perform well. Instead of focusing on what God had *said*—that they could take the land because He had given them victory—they focused on what they *saw*. Their poor thinking led to poor choices.

While good thoughts always support good choices, poor thoughts support poor choices. And poor choices always produce a poor life. In fact, the life you and I have right now is the result of the thoughts and choices we've made in the past. The way this process unfolds in a person's life is varied, but the pattern is as simple as basic math:

Our Thoughts + Our Choices = Our Outcome

41

Next-Level Concepts

You can only perform to the level of your thinking. Good thoughts always support good choices. The life you have right now is the result of the thoughts and choices you've made in the past.

HOW TO DEAL WITH POOR THINKING

If there's ever a place where poor thoughts have to be eliminated, it's in the field of sales. I've worked as an institutional sales director for a large investment advisory firm for more than seven years. During this time I have been one of the top salesmen in the company. However, this success has required me to engage in a military-style lockdown on my thoughts—especially when I was presented with opportunities for fear, doubt, and worry.

There were seasons when success seemed to elude me. I'd lose a big client or fail to win an important account, and immediately poor thoughts would try to take over. I'd hear, "You've lost your edge. Your season of success is over. How are you going to support your lifestyle if you can't win an account?"

The longer I entertained those thoughts, the more my performance was affected. So I had to make a choice: I could entertain the poor thoughts I was hearing or expel them from my thinking. I chose to expel them and replace them with healthy ones.

Realize that poor thoughts don't just go away. You can't wish them away, and thinking about other things only brings temporary relief. No, in order to get rid of poor thinking that robs you of peace and jeopardizes your future, you must screen your thoughts and then expel the ones that don't line up with what God says about you in His Word.

Next-Level Concepts

Poor thoughts don't just go away. To get
rid of them you must screen your thoughts
and expel the ones that don't line up with
what God says about you in His Word.

Think of it like the screening they do at the airport.
Everyone who wants to get a seat on an airplane must go
through a security screening to ensure they aren't carrying
anything dangerous that would jeopardize the flight. The
same principle applies to our thoughts. If you're carrying a
mind-set or belief that will jeopardize your journey to the
next level, it has to be removed.

Thank goodness Jesus showed us how. The Bible says that
on one particular occasion, the devil tempted Jesus with a
series of evil thoughts. One thing he told Jesus was that he
would give Him all the kingdoms of the earth if He would
simply bow down and submit to the devil's authority. The
thought must have been appealing to Jesus, or it wouldn't
have been a real temptation. However, Jesus rejected the
thought and said, "Get thee behind me, Satan: for it is written,
Thou shat worship the Lord thy God, and him only shalt thou
serve" (Luke 4:8, KJV).

Through Christ's example, we are given the major key
required to defeat poor thinking: *speak the truth of God's
Word against the enemy.* Jesus denied destructive thoughts
the opportunity to enter His heart by saying what is written
in Scripture. In other words, He said what God says. When
confronted with a poor thought, Jesus never remained silent.
Neither should we. We must speak to poor thoughts and
declare what's written in God's Word.

Next-Level Concepts

When confronted with a poor thought, never remain silent. Speak to poor thoughts and declare what's written in God's Word.

This is what I did. I had to speak to the poor thoughts of negativity and defeat before they gained a foothold in my life. I didn't just say positive words. I said what God says. I found a promise in the Word of God that I could truly believe, and then I spoke it. Of course, every word that God spoke in the Bible is true. However, the only one that will ever work for you is the one that *you* believe. I quoted God's promises about financial provision and confessed His favor over my life. I literally spoke to the geographic territory I was assigned, commanding it to respond and produce good fruit. Speaking to your sales territory, your bank account, or your business may sound crazy. But is it any crazier than listening to destructive thoughts of poverty and despair that are trying to sabotage your success and kill you? I don't think so. Clearly, the outcome of speaking God's Word over our lives is a whole lot better than just sitting silently and swallowing the thoughts of the enemy.

THOUGHTS AFFECT WORDS, AND WORDS AFFECT OUTCOMES

The reason we must take control of our thoughts is because they directly affect what comes out of our mouth. And what we say affects what we experience.

God gives us a very vivid illustration of the importance of watching our words in the life of a Jewish priest named Zechariah. Zechariah and his wife, Elizabeth, were both very old and had not been able to have children. However, one day while Zechariah was performing his ministerial duties in the temple, an angel appeared and gave him some great news.

> *The angel said, "Don't be afraid, Zechariah! God has heard your prayer. Your wife, Elizabeth, will give you a son, and you are to name him John."*
>
> —LUKE 1:13, NLT

Now, you have to remember that Zechariah and Elizabeth were way past the age of childbearing. They had desired children for years, but it seemed like it just wasn't meant to be. Then one day God showed up with an answer that not only seemed late but also impossible. "You're going to have a son," the angel said. But Zechariah just couldn't wrap his head around how it could possibly occur. His mind was hindered by poor thinking. "It's too late," he thought. "We're too old. Elizabeth's body just can't handle it." So out of the overflow of Zechariah's heart, he opened his mouth and said,

> *Do you expect me to believe this? I'm an old man and my wife is an old woman.*
>
> —LUKE 1:18, THE MESSAGE

I have to admit, the angel's message was hard to believe, given the circumstances. Of course, for an outside observer who has the benefit of knowing the end from the beginning, it's easy to say, "Where's your faith, Zechariah? God can do anything." However, Zechariah didn't know the end of the story. He simply thought the same thing you and I would have thought if we were told to believe the impossible. We would try to wrap our mind around it but find it very difficult.

Next-Level Concepts

The outcome of speaking God's Word over your life is a whole lot better than just sitting silently and swallowing the thoughts of the enemy. You must take control of your thoughts because they directly affect what you say and what you experience.

Think about it. What if your doctor has confirmed that you have terminal cancer, but a prophetic word comes forth in church in which God says He can heal people in the most dire of circumstances—including cancer? Which thought would you believe is more credible? Or perhaps your school tuition is due next week, and you have no money to pay for it. What's worse, you can't return to school unless it's paid. While the circumstances say it's impossible, God says in His Word that He will supply all your needs according to His riches in glory by Christ Jesus (Phil. 4:19). Like Zechariah, you now have to choose which word will dominate your thinking.

Unfortunately, Zechariah chose to focus on his circumstances. How did God respond to his words of doubt? We read:

> *Then the angel said, "I am Gabriel! I stand in the very presence of God. It was he who sent me to bring you this good news! But now, since you didn't believe what I said, you will be silent and unable to speak until the child is born. For my words will certainly be fulfilled at the proper time."*
>
> —Luke 1:19–20, nlt

In His mercy, God actually stopped Zechariah from speaking so that his mouth wouldn't hinder God's promise from coming to pass in his life. If Zechariah had continued to say what he thought instead of what God thought, he would have actually forfeited the very promise he so desperately desired.

Now contrast Zechariah's response with the response of Mary, the mother of Jesus. When Mary was still a virgin, the same angel who came to Zechariah also appeared to her with an even more preposterous thought. Scripture says...

> *The angel said to her, "Do not be afraid, Mary; for you have found favor with God. And behold, you will conceive in your womb and bear a son, and you shall name Him Jesus. He will be great and will be called the Son of the Most High; and the Lord God will give Him the throne of His father David; and He will reign over the house of Jacob forever, and His kingdom will have no end." Mary said to the angel, "How can this be, since I am a virgin?"*
> —LUKE 1:30–34, NASU

Now, you may be thinking, "Wait a minute. It's one thing to believe that an elderly couple can still have kids when they're past the age of childbearing. It's another thing entirely to believe a woman can have a child without ever having sex with a man. They didn't have in vitro fertilization back then!" All these thoughts have merit. So how do we wrap our head around what God said?

This is why Mary asked: "How can this be?" It's the same question Zechariah asked. They both were trying to figure it out in their heads. However, once the angel told Mary that the Holy Spirit would cause it to happen, she quit trying to figure it out and shut out all thoughts of doubt that were contrary to what God had said. Listen to her response:

> *Be it unto me according to thy word.*
> —LUKE 1:38, KJV

That's the key. Mary took control of her thoughts and chose to think what God was thinking and say what He was saying. We don't hear her say another word about "how" or "but" or "if only." She simply chose God's thoughts instead of poor thinking, and the outcome was victory—not just for her, but for all mankind.

So here's the lesson God wants you and me to learn: *don't entertain thoughts that are robbing you of peace and lying about the future He intends for you.* Cast them down by saying what God says. If sickness is gripping your body and is telling you to give up, ask the Holy Spirit to help you find a scripture that you can use to combat the attack of the enemy. You can declare His promises like those found in Exodus 23:25–26, Psalm 103:3, and 1 Peter 2:24. You don't have to accept death just because the thought of death comes into your mind. Likewise, if you think your marriage is beyond repair, speak against that thought by declaring God's Word on the issue. And if your children have turned to a life of darkness, speak against those fearful thoughts of their being lost by declaring God's Word over their lives.

Next-Level Concepts

Don't entertain thoughts that are robbing you of peace and lying about the future God intends for you. Cast them down by saying what God says in His Word.

Remember, these situations may seem impossible, but "with God *all things* are possible!" (Matt. 19:26, emphasis added). Get rid of poor thinking. Find out what God says about your situation in His Word and declare it over your life. As you do, you will position yourself to do better than ever!

NEXT-LEVEL ACTION STEPS

1. What poor thoughts are you confronted with most often?

_____

_____

_____

_____

2. Using a Bible concordance, search the Scriptures and find at least two promises from God's Word that combat these poor thoughts. Commit these to memory and speak them out loud whenever the enemy tries to get you to think poor thoughts.

_____

_____

_____

_____

3. Like the Israelites, does it seem as if something or someone is preventing you from entering your "promised land"? If so, describe the situation. What can you learn and apply in your life from what happened to Israel?

_____

_____

_____

_____

4. Both Zechariah and Mary had a promise from God through the angel Gabriel, but each responded differently. What can you learn and apply in your own life from these examples?

_____

_____

Activity for Advancement: Clearly, having the Word of God filling your heart and mind and ready on your tongue is a major key to victory over poor thinking! In what practical ways can you get more of God's Word in you on a daily basis? Pray and ask the Lord for His input. His ideas are life changing!

Scriptures for Meditation: Hebrews 4:12; Colossians 3:16; 2 Timothy 3:16–17

THE POWER OF DIVINE DESIGN

ETTING RID OF poor thinking will make it easier to leave your current level of living. However, you will need to do more than think right in order to reach the status of "better than ever." Like the space shuttle *Endeavor*, you will also need power! Fortunately God has an abundant supply. He's given us the power of prayer, the power of love, and the power of faith. There's power in our praise and power in forgiveness. However, in this chapter I'd like to focus on the power of divine design.

YOU ARE GIFTED BY GOD!

Every person born on the planet has been gifted by God with a unique design, and you are no exception. Your gifting not only sets you apart from others but also gives you the ability, if released, to affect your level of living. I call this an endowment of God's grace. Grace is like a heavenly toolkit that is placed on the inside of you, enabling you to produce the type of life you were meant to live. The Bible confirms this truth saying:

> *God has given different gifts to each of us.*
> —1 CORINTHIANS 7:7, CEV

> *For we are God's workmanship, created in Christ Jesus to do good works, which God prepared in advance for us to do.*
> —EPHESIANS 2:10

Isn't that amazing? Long before you ever showed up on the planet, God had a plan for your life. He personally created you with certain gifts, traits, and qualities to help you get your job done.

Next-Level Concepts

Every person born on the planet has been gifted by God with a unique design, and you are no exception. I call this an endowment of God's grace.

Consider Michael Phelps, the young Olympic phenomenon who won an eye-popping eight gold medals at the 2008 Olympics. His physical attributes helped him become the greatest swimmer the world has ever seen. In fact, you could say that Michael was born to swim. He's 6 feet 4 inches tall and is double-jointed in both his chest area and ankles.[6] This enables him to raise his arms higher above his head than most swimmers and increase the efficiency of his starts and turns in the water. It also allows his feet, which are size 14, to function like flippers, giving him a clear advantage.[7]

If that weren't enough, Phelps has a lung capacity that is twice that of normal humans, and his muscles produce nearly 50 percent less lactic acid than normal, enabling him to work harder and longer than many of his competitors. His arm span is also unique. If he were to stretch both his arms in opposite directions, the distance would cover 6 feet 7 inches—a full three inches greater than his height.[8] This allows him to propel his body through the water as if he had two oars in his hand. In fact, according to his coach, Bob Bowman, Phelps can cover a distance of twenty-five yards in just six to eight strokes. The average freestyle swimmer needs at least twelve to sixteen strokes to cover the same distance.[9] These features, combined with his long torso, big hands, and endless energy (he was diagnosed with ADHD at the age of nine) give Phelps real power in the water—so much power that he's able to produce results that are exceedingly, abundantly above what most people think is possible.

Of course, when you use an example like Michael Phelps to describe the power of gifting, people can't help but think he's the exception. Yes, he is special. But so are you. God has given different gifts to each of us. This means no one's been left out. Everyone from a world-class swimmer to the homeless man on the street has been blessed with an endowment of grace.

This fact was marvelously demonstrated in a late 2010 story about a man named Ted Williams. Mr. Williams was a homeless man who practically lived on the corner of I-71 and Hudson Street in Cleveland, Ohio. Every day he would stand in the same spot, begging for money and any handouts that a passerby was willing to give. He held up a cardboard sign that read:

> *I have a god-given gift of voice. I'm an ex-radio announcer who has fallen on hard times. Please! Any help will be gratefully appreciated. Thank you and God bless. Happy holidays.*[10]

I'm not sure how many days Williams carried that sign around with him. However, one day someone important took notice. It was a *Columbus Dispatch* reporter and videographer who happened to be in the area. He pulled up to the corner where Williams was panhandling and said, "We're going to make you work for your dollar. Say something with that great radio voice." I'm sure those reporters weren't expecting much, perhaps a raspy old voice or some feeble excuse. Yet when Ted Williams opened his mouth, a gift that can only come from God emerged: "When you're listening to nothing but the best of oldies...you're listening to Magic 98.9."

Wow! His delivery was as smooth as butter. In fact, it was so smooth that the reporters decided to put a video of Williams and his "golden voice" on YouTube. In a matter of days, the video went viral, causing offers for voice-overs to stream in from all around the world. The Cleveland Cavaliers called him. NFL Films wanted him for their documentaries. And Kraft Foods wanted him for commercials. Keep in mind this was a man who was broke, homeless, and rejected by society. He was living far beneath the ability and power that resided within him. However, once his gift was released for others to witness, it caused everyone to stand up and take notice.

Next-Level Concepts

God has given different gifts to each of us. No one's been left out. Everyone from world-class swimmers to the homeless man on the street has been blessed with an endowment of grace.

Find and Refine Your Gift

I'm using the stories of Phelps and Williams to emphasize my point because they are so different from each other. Yet the key that opened the door for both of them was the same—their gift. Both men found a way to make their gifting a strength in their lives, and they aren't alone.

After interviewing thousands of people in many different fields of study, the authors of the book *Now, Discover Your Strength* found that people who identify and then build their life around their gift are some of the most successful and fulfilled people in the world. They explain:

> *Whenever you interview people who are truly successful at their chosen profession—from teaching*

*to telemarketing, acting to accounting—you discover
that the secret to their success lies in their ability to
discover their strengths and then organize their life
so that these strengths can be applied.*[11]

In other words, the power to live better than ever can be found in your gifting. All you have to do is find it and refine it.

And it's not as difficult as you might think. Finding your gift begins by asking yourself a few important questions. First, what do other people consistently commend you for? For example, do people commend you for your speaking ability? Do they comment about how competitive you are? Maybe you're the "recognized expert" when it comes to understanding computers. Whatever traits other people consistently recognize in you is a good clue as to what your gifts are.

Here's another good indicator of your gifts. What do people often come to you for help with? For example, creative people are always called upon to come up with innovative ideas. When others can't figure out how to create or communicate a concept, creative people usually come up with a solution. They say, "What if we did this?" Similarly, people who have relationship gifts are often asked to help connect other people. They always seem to know someone who knows someone. Then there are people with motivational gifts. They are called upon to bring encouragement, vision, and hope to others. Ministers, counselors, and coaches often possess this gift. In fact, the need for motivation is so great today that it's grown into a multi-billion dollar industry annually.

Next-Level Concepts

The power to get to your next level can be found in your gifting. All you have to do is find it and refine it.

Are you beginning to identify the gift(s) God has given you? If not, take a few moments and write down three things that people commend you for and/or consistently ask you for help with. To help you uncover your gifts, read through these sentences, completing each phrase with words that best apply to you. "People often look to me for _____." "People depend upon me to _____." "My friends always ask me to help them _____."

Three things people commend me for or ask me to help them with are:

1. _____

2. _____

3. _____

WHAT ARE YOU PASSIONATE ABOUT?

Your passion will usually draw you to your purpose and identify the gift you will need to accomplish it. For example, Dr. Martin Luther King Jr. was passionate about freedom and justice. This led him to a life dedicated to helping the oppressed and speaking on behalf of those who couldn't speak for themselves. It also required gifts of compassion, communication, and leadership. Bill Gates was passionate about creating new technologies that redefined the way people work and play. This led him to creating the most powerful operating system in the world and uncovered his analytical and creative gifting. Others are passionate about educating children, freeing victims of human trafficking, or helping people live healthier lives. Each of these passions will require specific endowments of grace to be accomplished.

Take a moment and identify three of your greatest passions. For example, "I am passionate about creating beautiful music," or "I am passionate about holding elected officials accountable for their actions," or "I am passionate about saving the spiritually lost." Next to your passions, list the traits you think are needed to accomplish them.

Three of my greatest passions in life are:

1. _____

2. _____

3. _____

WHAT DO YOU FIND YOURSELF TRYING TO FIX?

This is another good question to answer. Said differently, what bothers you greatly, or what do you want to help others with the most? For example, beauticians want to fix unruly hair. Personal trainers want to change unhealthy lifestyles and teachers want to eradicate illiteracy.

By identifying what you want to help others fix or do, you can find what you have been called and gifted to fix. For instance, people who have the gift of organization need to either fix or leave environments that are consistently unorganized. They have a hard time working with people, processes, and organizations that have no sense of order. Similarly, people with a gift of compassion feel the need to help others who are hurting. While other people can go to sleep after seeing a television report on child abuse, a person with a gift of compassion will stay up for hours wondering why nothing is being done to fix the problem or trying to determine what they can do to help.

Take a moment and list three things that frustrate you to the point of taking action. To help you in your search, read through these sentences, completing each with words that apply to you. "I am very frustrated when _____." "I hate the fact that no one is addressing the needs of _____." "If I could fix anything in the world around me, the thing I would fix would be _____." Along with these things, list the traits you think are needed to get the job done.

Three things that frustrate me most or I want to fix are:

1. _____

2. _____

3. _____

WHAT DO YOU LOVE TO DO?

This is the final question you should ask yourself. Think about it. What activities brings you joy? Since love is one of the most powerful motivators God created, it's not surprising that He would use love to draw you toward your gifting and purpose. For example, Bill Gates loved technology and computers so much that he spent hours creating new programs. Warren Buffett's love for investing led him to be one of the most successful investors of all time. In case after case, this principle holds true. It's the things you love most that help identify your gifting and lead you to your purpose.

This is not to say that God doesn't call us to things that we, at first, don't love. Sometimes, at the onset, we might even hate what we are called to do. However, love and joy must eventually be present in order to complete the assignment. Come to think of it, I don't know anyone who is operating consistently at a higher level without a love for what they do. Great preachers love studying the Word of God. Great basketball players love playing ball. Great musicians love creating music and performing. If a person stops loving what they do, there is a good chance they aren't doing it as well as they used to or they are ready for a change.

Take a moment and write down three things you love to do. Examples include, "I love reading great fiction books." "I love working with animals." "I love being around children."

Three things I love to do are:

1. _____
2. _____
3. _____

Armed with information from these four questions, place your answers in the circles provided. They represent what Lance Wallnau calls your "gift cluster" and are, by definition, the "ingredients" you can use to produce life on a new, higher level.

Now, as any chef will tell you, ingredients alone don't make a meal. They have to be prepared, combined, stirred, and placed in the right environment for a specific length of time before you can benefit from them. The same is true with your gift cluster. In order to produce the kind of power necessary to achieve new levels of living, you must turn these gifts into a strength you can use in your everyday life. This is where the power of practice comes in, which is the next important step.

Your Gift Cluster

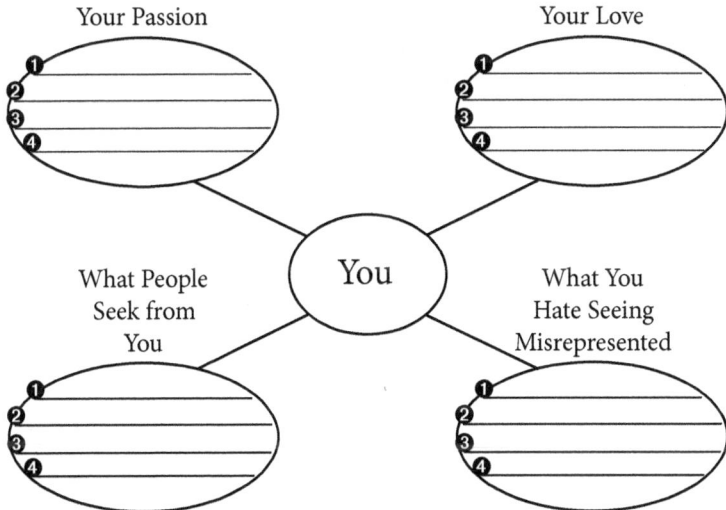

Your Passion

Your Love

You

What People Seek from You

What You Hate Seeing Misrepresented

NEXT-LEVEL ACTION STEPS

1. From all the info you've gathered, what would you say are your top three gifts?

_____

_____

_____

2. Do you feel your gifts are important? Why or why not? Stop and think. What would the world be like if *no one* had your gifts? What vital things would be missing?

_____

_____

_____

_____

_____

3. Are you actively using these gifts and talents? If so, how and where?

_____

_____

_____

_____

4. What is something you can do *weekly* to help develop your gifts? How about *daily*? Are there books you feel you should read and DVDs you feel you should watch? Seminars or classes you feel led to take?

_____

_____

Activity for Advancement: When it comes to gifts and talents, one of the traps we often fall into is comparing and competing with others—even becoming jealous and envious of their gifts. Are you struggling with this? If so, pray and ask God to forgive you and give you an appreciation for the gifts in others. Lastly, *speak a blessing* on the person(s) you have been jealous of. This will open the door of God's blessing upon your own life.

Scriptures for Meditation: Romans 12:3–8; 1 Corinthians 12:4–31; Matthew 25:14–30

THE POWER OF PRACTICE

THE SUCCESS MICHAEL Phelps gained at the 2008 Olympics was made possible, in part, by the natural endowments he possessed. However, it wasn't only big feet, big lungs, or an enormous wingspan that turned a possibility of Olympic history into a reality for Phelps. It was also how he perfected the gift he was given. More specifically, Phelps broke through to new levels of athletic achievement by consistently practicing. Day after day, he trained for the level of success he hoped to achieve. This meant five-hour workouts six days a week. It also meant swimming a greater distance each day than most people commute to work. Phelps understood that if he wanted to achieve a new level of Olympic performance, he couldn't rely on gifting alone. He would have to practice. In fact, practice was so important to him that he did it 365 days a year.

Phelps isn't alone in his reliance on practice. In case after case, we find that people who did extraordinary things spent years practicing what they hoped to accomplish. Even the once-homeless man Ted Williams spent time practicing as a mid-day radio announcer in the 1980s. So it's not just gifting that brings success. Practice must be present. The more we practice the gift we've been given, the more we are able to make the extraordinary look normal.

Next-Level Concepts

People who do extraordinary things spend
weeks, months, and years practicing what they
hope to accomplish. It's not just gifting that
brings success. Practice must be present.

Take five-time NBA champion Kobe Bryant. In an interview with *Men's Fitness* magazine, Bryant emphasized that practice is the thing that makes what should be difficult, easy. He said:

> *The thing that I tell them (other young players)
> all the time is consistency. If they watch me train,
> running on a track, it doesn't look like I'm over-
> exerting myself. It's a consistency with which you do
> it; in other words, it's an every-day-thing. You have
> a program, and a schedule, and you have to abide
> by that, religiously. You just stick to it, and it's the
> consistency that pays off.*[12]

The key word here is *daily*. Regardless of what you're gifted to do, you have to daily put it to use in order to get the most out of it. Consider Tiger Woods. Here is a snapshot of what his daily routine looked like when he was dominating the PGA:

- **6:30 a.m.** – One hour of cardio. Choice between endurance runs, sprints, or biking.

- **7:30 a.m.** – One hour of lower weight training. 60–70 percent of normal lifting weight, high reps, and multiple sets.

- **8:30 a.m.** – High protein/low-fat breakfast. Typically includes egg-white omelet with vegetables.

- **9:00 a.m.** – Two hours on the golf course. Hit on the range and work on swing.

- **11:00 a.m.** – Practice putting for thirty minutes to an hour.

- **Noon** - Play nine holes.

- **1:30 p.m.** – High protein/low-fat lunch. Typically includes grilled chicken or fish, salad, and vegetables.

- **2:00 p.m.** – Three to four hours on the golf course. Work on swing and short game, and occasionally play another nine holes.

- **6:30 p.m.** – Thirty minutes of upper weight training. High reps.

- **7:00 p.m.** – Dinner and rest.[13]

What's amazing is that Tiger has been blessed with tremendous athletic ability. Yet he understands that gifting is never an assurance of success. Practice is the thing that makes your gift come alive.

Next-Level Concepts

Gifting is never an assurance of success. Practice is the thing that makes your gift come alive. You have to daily put it to use in order to get the most out of it.

The Benefit of Practice

Even nature testifies to the importance of practice when trying to reach the next level. For example, the butterfly is a beautiful and graceful insect. But it doesn't start out that way. Every butterfly begins as a caterpillar—a mere hairy-looking worm. However, on the inside of that worm is a gifting that's unlike anything else in nature. To see it released, the caterpillar has to practice daily. Every day, while it's in its cocoon, it must work to break through the tough shell that keeps it bound in its current state. Every day it has to push and push, as if in training, to reach its next level.

To the casual observer, the caterpillar's efforts may seem futile. Yet his daily training routine is doing more for him than just helping him break free from what's constraining him. It's also allowing him to build the crucial muscle mass needed to sustain life at the next level as a butterfly. In fact, if the caterpillar were freed from his cocoon by outside forces, he would never develop the muscle strength needed to sustain life as a butterfly. If he never practiced using what he had been given while in his cocoon, he would never reach his full potential. However, if daily training is allowed to run its course, the caterpillar will transform into the beautiful butterfly God intended it to be. It will produce results that are exceedingly, abundantly above what it was able to do in the past.

Again, the key to turning your gifting into a strength is practice. The Bible clearly supports the idea of practice. Consider the following verses:

> *But those who don't put into practice what they hear are like a person who built a house without a foundation. The floodwater smashed against it and it collapsed instantly. It was completely destroyed.*
> —Luke 6:49, CES, EMPHASIS ADDED

In his grace, God has given us different gifts for doing certain things well. So if God has given you the ability to prophesy, speak out with as much faith as God has given you. If your gift is serving others, serve them well. If you are a teacher, teach well. If your gift is to encourage others, be encouraging. If it is giving, give generously. If God has given you leadership ability, take the responsibility seriously. And if you have a gift for showing kindness to others, do it gladly.

—ROMANS 12:6–8, NLT, EMPHASIS ADDED

Notice the emphasis on using what you've been given. Prophets are told to practice prophesying, givers are encouraged to practice giving, and encouragers are commanded to practice encouraging. This is how you turn your gift into a strength—you practice it.

So if cooking is your gift, perfect it. Go to culinary school; create a cookbook. If you're gifted at creative writing, begin writing short stories. Participate in workshops, and submit your material in contests. Don't let the gift that God gave you remain hidden. Dr. Ed Cole, a pioneer in men's ministry, said it best: "The degree to which you practice in private is the degree to which you will perform in public."[14] The Navy Seals say it a little different: "The more you sweat in peacetime, the less you will bleed in war."

Next-Level Concepts

Don't let the gift God gave you remain hidden. Develop it. It's only after you master what you've been given that you become qualified to enter another level of living.

The Old Testament saint David serves as a great example of this truth. He didn't gain access to the king's palace just because a prophet anointed him with oil. He gained access because of what he practiced—the gift of music and the art of fighting. The Bible says that David was selected to enter the palace because of the way he played the harp. In fact, he played so skillfully that whenever an evil spirit was tormenting King Saul, it would leave. (See 1 Samuel 16:4–23.)

Scripture also records David's fearless and formidable fighting ability. When the Israelite army ran from Goliath, it was David's skillful use of the sling that made him stand out. Of course, when David first told King Saul he would go and fight the giant, Saul thought he was crazy. However, David had spent years out in the wilderness in training. He had killed big, scary creatures like lions and bears, and his weapon of choice was a sling.

Unfortunately, most people have been taught that the sling David used to fight Goliath was a child's toy. Some also think he used a small pebble that he found in the stream to hurl at the giant's head. But that was not the case. The sling was recognized as a powerful weapon in the hand of a warrior during David's time. And they didn't use pebbles. They used rocks the size of baseballs and hurled them with great accuracy. The Bible says that among Benjamin's elite troops, a division of Israel's army, seven hundred were left-handed, and each of them could sling a rock and hit a target within a hairsbreadth without missing. (See Judges 20:16.) So when David faced Goliath, he wasn't hoping things would go well. He knew they would. All he needed was an opportunity to get off one good shot, and the Lord gave him that chance. When the rock left David's sling, it was moving at such a high speed that it literally became lodged in Goliath's skull. Cutting off his head was just a formality.

David achieved a new level of success that day because he practiced. Ironically, the outcome of the battle could have been completely different. When David first came to King Saul, Saul tried to get David to wear his armor. David quickly realized it wouldn't work and decided to use the weapon he was most familiar with—the slingshot. Scripture says:

> *Saul put his battle tunic on David; he put a bronze helmet on David's head and dressed him in armor. David fastened Saul's sword over his clothes and tried to walk, but he had never practiced doing this. "I can't walk in these things," David told Saul. "I've never had any practice doing this." So David took all those things off.*
> —1 SAMUEL 17:38–39, GW, EMPHASIS ADDED

David realized that he couldn't achieve the level of success he wanted by trying to do something he had not practiced. Neither can we. We can't secure a job promotion without practicing an exemplary work ethic. We can't achieve weight loss without practicing discipline regarding what we eat, and we can't build stronger relationships without practicing forgiveness and love. No matter how we might attempt to get around this truth, we can't. It's derived from an irrefutable law that cannot be changed or denied. You can't consistently produce in public what you won't practice in private.

Next-Level Concepts

Unless you consistently practice what you hope to achieve, your chances of securing it are very remote. Practice refines your gift and releases its power.

BY DEFAULT OR DESIGN—IT'S YOUR CHOICE

Hopefully you're starting to see the correlation between what we practice and what we experience in life. The result is what Amber Riviere, founder of Rock Your Genius, calls either a "life by design" or a "life by default."[15] I think we all know what a life by default looks like. It means your choices are limited and you live on someone else's terms. You take vacations by permission, receive raises only when available, and make choices only after others have chosen first. This doesn't sound like next-level living to me.

On the other hand, those who daily practice what they plan to produce don't live by default. They live by design and are therefore able to create the future they want as opposed to living with what's been doled out to them. Again, the key word here is *daily*. Practice on purpose what you want to produce. Daily go to the gym. Daily tell your spouse you love them. Daily encourage your children. Daily pray. Daily read God's Word. Consistency is a major key to victory.

PRACTICE DELIBERATELY

In addition to practicing daily is practicing deliberately. Geoff Colvin, author of the national best-selling book *Talent Is Overrated,* masterfully explained the term "deliberate practice" using the game of golf. He stated:

> *Simply hitting a bucket of balls is not deliberate practice, which is why most golfers don't get better. Hitting an eight-iron 300 times with a goal of leaving the ball within 20 feet of the pin 80 percent of the time, continually observing results and making appropriate adjustments, and doing that for hours every day—that's deliberate practice.[16]*

The power of deliberate practice is nothing short of amazing. Studies show that it can produce results that are exceedingly, abundantly above what's imaginable. For example, Colvin describes a study conducted at Carnegie Mellon University where researchers verbally gave a random series of numbers to students and then asked them to repeat the numbers in the order they heard them. It's important to note that none of the students who participated in the study possessed extraordinary memories. They were ordinary people who, like most of us, have to focus just to remember a new phone number they hear. Yet in this study, students specifically trained over and over again to recall a very large series of numbers. After testing for one hour a day for several days, some students could recall fourteen numbers! Over time and with additional training, students were able to recall even more. One student was able to recall eighty-two digits!

Imagine someone randomly giving you eighty-two digits and then asking you to repeat them in order. Now, that's an exceedingly, abundantly above memory. However, what's truly amazing about these results is not the volume of numbers the students remembered, but who was doing the remembering. These were ordinary, average people like you and me who normally couldn't remember a statistically significant number of digits. Yet the power to remember more than they could think or imagine was inside of them. So, what was the difference? How did they obtain such a high level of recall? According to those conducting the study, they spent over two hundred hours of focused, deliberate practice, memorizing numbers for a period of two years to generate these types of results.[17]

Next-Level Concepts

The power of deliberate practice is nothing short of amazing. Those who daily and deliberately practice what they plan to produce don't live by default. They live by design and are therefore able to create the future they want.

I decided to test the power of deliberate practice by using a very unscientific experiment of my own. My test subjects were my own kids, ages ten and twelve, and the skill for which I tested them was paddleball. Most of us have played with a paddleball at some point in our lives. It looks like a Ping-Pong paddle except it has an elastic string and ball attached to it. My kids had never used one, so they were far from proficient. When they first started playing with it, they could only hit the ball consecutively about five or six times. However, after an hour or so of practice throughout the day, I noticed a change. They got better.

Within just a few days of focused practice, they were able to hit the ball more than thirty times without missing the paddle. After a period of five days and what had to be at least seven hours of practice, they could hit the ball more than one hundred thirty times without missing a beat! Were they natural-born paddleball hitters? Of course not. However, they trained for a specific goal—they watched a video of other people successfully doing it and spent hours of deliberate practice, trying to do the same thing. Although they weren't experts, in time they were performing better than ever. That's the power of deliberate practice.

So, what would happen if we applied this same principle to the areas of our lives in which we wanted to go to the next level? What if we consistently and deliberately practiced telling our spouse and children that we loved them? What if we did something every week to make each day easier and more enjoyable for them? What if we practiced listening better or giving them more encouragement? I believe we would experience new levels of fulfillment in our marriages and relationships.

The good news is that this principle can be applied to our jobs, our health, our finances, and everything else in our lives. Think about it. What if we deliberately practiced getting to work on time? What if we deliberately limited our carbohydrate intake after 7:00 p.m. and exercised daily? How would our health change if we practiced reducing our salt intake? What if we deliberately practiced saving a portion of what we earned each week? I believe if we did these things, we would begin to see a great surge of power show up on our behalf—power strong enough to lift us from one level of existence to the next. In the next chapter, I'll introduce you to that power.

NEXT-LEVEL ACTION STEPS

1. Write down three specific goals for your life—areas in which you want to go to the next level. It could be your health, marriage, job, relationship with God, or some other goals.

_____

_____

_____

_____

_____

2. Is there something you know in your heart you can deliberately do daily to see your goals come about? If so, what is it? Pray and ask God for His input.

_____

_____

_____

_____

3. Would you say you are living more by default or design? What things in your life cause you to come to this conclusion?

_____

_____

_____

_____

4. What behaviors are you deliberately practicing that you would like to stop?

_____

_____

_____

_____

_____

Activity for Advancement: Experts agree that it takes about twenty-one days (three weeks) to develop a new habit. Think about it. Deliberately doing something for twenty-one days will carve out a new groove of behavior in your life. What healthy habit would you really like to see formed? Is it exercise? Reading a book a half hour a day? Going to bed and getting up at a set time? Put the principle of deliberate practice to the test. Commit to faithfully doing what you want to see formed in your life for twenty-one days and watch what happens. The results just might amaze you!

Scriptures for Meditation: 1 Timothy 4:7–8; Hebrews 5:13–14; 1 Peter 1:13–16.

THE POWER OF GRACE AND FAVOR

Accord ing to Malcom Gladwell, author of the *New York Times* best-selling book *Outliers*, people don't achieve new levels of performance by talent alone. Instead, the path to success is paved by something much more complex—privilege, resources, and, most importantly, work. Ten thousand hours of it, to be exact.

Based upon research conducted by Dr. Daniel Levitin, Mr. Gladwell found that if you wholly dedicate yourself to a specific task for ten thousand hours, which is approximately seven to ten years, not only can you accomplish anything, but you can also *master* it. You can literally go to the next level. This is great news for people who have a lot of time on their hands. However, what can you do if you want to get to the next level before the year 2020? That's where grace and favor come in.

Grace is God's ability to do what would otherwise be impossible. It is supernatural power to help you do what technically can't be done, given your resources, time, and ability. Similarly, favor is the release of God's goodwill on your life. Let me give you an example from my own life to illustrate what I mean. In the late 1990s, I used to work as manager within the accounting department of a large brokerage firm. While I saw a measured level of success in this role, the job never made a real demand on the ability God placed inside of me. Then one day I heard about an opportunity that opened up within the investment department of the firm. The position would not only allow me to learn about investing (which seemed much more appealing to me) but would also give me the opportunity to teach others and interface with clients.

There was only one problem. Actually, two. First, I had absolutely no experience in the field of investments. Second, my current salary was based upon a manager's tenure, not someone seeking an entry-level position in finance. I remember the interview to this day. I was sitting across the table from the head of the department as he looked over my résumé, trying to figure out why I even applied for the job. He was polite but direct: "I think we're looking for someone with a little more experience, Mr. Woods."

All I could tell him was that if he was willing to invest his time to teach me the job, I would work incredibly hard to ensure that he received a return on his investment. He smiled, and that was the end of the interview.

However, a few weeks later, the company went into a serious cost-cutting mode and put a freeze on all hiring. The only the exception were candidates who were already employees of the firm. Little did I realize that the "freeze" perfectly coincided with the investment department's attempt to fill the position I sought. They were stuck. They had an opening but were prevented from hiring an external candidate they really liked. Then it dawned them: "What about that guy who came in a few weeks ago? Maybe we can teach him the job."

I received a call a few weeks later, and the job was mine. Now, that's grace. God literally closed the door on all hiring within the entire firm until I was placed in the exact spot He desired for me. Incidentally, as soon as I was hired, the freeze was lifted. I would ultimately become a manager in that department and be sent around the country to help train financial advisors and service large institutional relationships. Believe me, I could have never in a million years orchestrated those events. Think about it. I was given a job that I was not qualified for, beat out other candidates with greater experience, and rewarded with a pay scale that went above and beyond what I deserved. Praise God for His grace.

It's the power to do what can't be done, given your own skill, resources, and ability.

The most powerful example of grace is our salvation. The Bible says we are saved by grace through faith (Eph. 2:8). In other words, it is impossible for us to get to heaven based upon our talent, effort, or resources. We aren't good enough, strong enough, or smart enough to earn our salvation on our own. However, the moment we receive God's grace in our life, we receive power to do what we can't do on our own. Grace makes righteousness available to us. Faith is simply the channel, or tool, we use to access grace.

Isn't grace amazing? It's what showed up in Ted Williams's life that fateful day in Cleveland, Ohio, and propelled him to a new level of living. Grace is what enables a real-estate agent to have her best year ever, even when all her colleagues are struggling. Grace is why a salesman can have a breakout year even though he doesn't make the best presentations. Grace will cause one church to double in size while others are falling like dominoes. And grace will enable a person to master his gift in considerably less time than the ten thousand hours it would normally take. Indeed, when grace is combined with our gifting and a regimen of focused practice, it produces what I call a perfect storm of next-level results.

Next-Level Concepts

Grace is God's ability to do what would otherwise be impossible. It's supernatural power to help you do what technically can't be done with your resources, time, and ability.

A Perfect Storm of Results

In meteorology, a perfect storm is a series of independent events that converge to generate results that are exponentially more powerful than what any single event could be on its own. I believe this is what happens when gifting, practice, and grace come together. It produces results that are exceedingly, abundantly above anything you can think or imagine.

Jennifer Hudson serves as a great illustration. For those who've never heard of Ms. Hudson, she is the celebrity face on the Weight Watcher commercials that air frequently on television. Where did she get her start? It was during the third season of the popular television show *American Idol*.

If you follow the show, you may remember that Ms. Hudson was the sixth finalist to be eliminated during the competition. As a result, her future in the entertainment business looked shaky at best. Prior contestants who finished in a similar position did get a chance to tour with the show, but few ever saw lasting musical success. Yet for Jennifer, her God-given ability and the years of practice she had invested in her gift were combined with an invisible, yet powerful, third element called favor. Favor took her early elimination, which the enemy meant for evil and should have been disastrous, and turned it around for her good.

Favor did for Jennifer what she couldn't do for herself. Although she lost on *American Idol* because she couldn't secure enough fans to vote for her, God's favor opened a door of unimaginable opportunity. Favor caused one man named Clive Davis—a powerful music executive—to cast his vote for her, and it changed her life forever. In the eight years since leaving *American Idol*, no contestant has ever done what Hudson has been able to accomplish: win an Oscar, a Golden Globe, and a BAFTA (British Academy of Film, Television and Art) Award. Hudson also won a Grammy and is the first African American singer to ever grace the cover of *Vogue* magazine.[18] Most recently, she completed her second album, which has been well received in the industry. Only the combination of gifting, practice, and favor can achieve such a perfect storm of results.

GRACE IS NOT LUCK

Let me be clear. The events that occurred in Jennifer Hudson's life were not the result of chance. She was not fortunate or lucky. In fact, on the night America was casting votes for their favorite *American Idol* contestant, a freakish storm knocked out phone lines in Jennifer's hometown of Chicago, thereby impacting the number of people who could even vote for her. Does that sound like luck to you? Clearly, luck had nothing to do with the blessings that ultimately came Jennifer's way.

Luck, by definition, is a series of events that are beyond control and completely dependent on chance. Grace and favor, on the other hand, is power that's under the full control of God and is specifically designed to generate results in your life that are unexplainable, unimaginable, and inconceivable. Doesn't that sound like what happened to Jennifer? Doesn't that sound like what happened to me?

Now, here's the good part. The same grace that was activated in my life can be activated in your life. The same power that helped Jennifer can help you. Do you believe it? I'm not saying you're going to be featured on the cover of *Vogue* or star in a major motion picture. However, when you allow grace to operate in your life, three things will always show up: the exceeding, the abundant, and the above.

Let me give you another example, this time from the life of the apostle Peter. The Bible says that prior to joining Jesus's ministry, Peter owned a fishing business. He had spent his entire life fishing on the shores of Gennesaret, perfecting and honing his skills. And he was good at what he did.

However, on one particular night of fishing, even Peter's best efforts failed to produce any results. He and his crew had spent the entire night dragging their nets on the floor of the lake, but they caught nothing.

In the morning, as they were cleaning their nets and getting ready to go home, Jesus entered the scene. Actually, you could say grace entered the scene because grace and truth come through Jesus. Seeing the men at work, grace (Jesus) asked if He could come aboard and use Peter's boat as podium to preach to the people. Now, think about what Jesus asked. Peter had been fishing all night and didn't catch a thing. I'm sure in the natural he was saying to himself, "Dude, I'm tired, smelly, and hungry. I just want to go home!" Yet out of respect for the anointing on Jesus's life, Peter agreed to let grace (Jesus) come aboard and then go fishing once again. And that's when a perfect storm of results burst forth. (See Luke 5:1–7.)

Peter's fishing ability and experience combined with the grace of God produced results that were almost unimaginable. The Bible says once grace (Jesus) got into the boat, Peter and his men caught so many fish that their nets were about to break, and the boat almost sank! In fact, they caught so many fish they had to ask for help to keep from drowning. Trust me, this was no ordinary day of fishing. What was Peter's response to this perfect storm of results? Scripture says he fell on his knees and "was gripped with bewildering amazement [allied to terror], and all who were with him, at the haul of fish which they had made" (Luke 5:9, AMP).

What kind of haul could possibly make a man who has fished his entire life become utterly befuddled? I can tell you what kind: a next-level kind—one that is exceedingly, abundantly above that he could imagine.

Next-Level Concepts

When gifting, practice, and God's grace come together, a perfect storm of results bursts forth—results that are exceedingly, abundantly above anything you can think or imagine.

HOW TO BRING GRACE ON BOARD

The kind of results Peter experienced that morning had nothing to do with luck. Peter's talent and experience couldn't even account for what happened on that day. Remember, he had been fishing all night and didn't catch anything. Yet when grace, talent, and practice met together, a new level of fishing emerged. All three had to be on board to produce results that were better than ever. So think about the area in your life that you'd like to raise to a new level. Are you gifted and capable in this area? Next, are you practicing and perfecting, on a daily basis, the goal you want to achieve? If so, all that's now required is grace.

Fortunately, God has an ample supply. However, He doesn't just randomly dish it out. The grace of God always comes for a reason. The Bible says clearly:

> *God is able to make all grace (every favor and earthly blessing) come to you in abundance, so that you may always and under all circumstances and whatever the need be self-sufficient [possessing enough to require no aid or support and furnished in abundance for every good work and charitable donation].*
> —2 CORINTHIANS 9:8, AMP, EMPHASIS ADDED

This verse reveals that if we have a God-given work to accomplish, which we all do, then we are eligible to receive

God's grace. In other words, when you live in accordance with your God-given purpose, you position yourself to receive the grace you need to accomplish your purpose. This is why I believed I received the job in the investment department. I was right where God wanted me to be.

Grace is always available in the place where God is calling you. Here's an example to illustrate what I mean. When Nehemiah, an Old Testament cupbearer to a foreign king, heard his people were living in the burnt remains of Jerusalem, the Bible says that he cried for days at the thought of his countrymen's plight. Day after day the Spirit of God moved on his heart to somehow find a way to help God's people. God was clearly calling him back to Jerusalem. However, there were things standing in his way. First and foremost, he was stuck in Persia. The second obstacle for Nehemiah was that he didn't have the resources to help anyone. And last but not least, he had no means to get back to Jerusalem. Indeed, the situation seemed impossible...until grace stepped in.

God set up a situation in which the king initiated conversation with Nehemiah. (No one was allowed to approach the king unless summoned. The consequence for doing so without permission was death.) One day the king noticed Nehemiah was sad and not his normal, peaceful self. He asked Nehemiah what was wrong, and Nehemiah shared his heart. Through this encounter Nehemiah was able to ask for permission to go and help his people. By God's grace, the king responded favorably in monumental proportions. Not only did he let Nehemiah journey back to his homeland, but he also financed the entire trip. He paid for all the supplies and reconstruction of the city and even built Nehemiah a house to live in while he was there. Can you imagine that?

This would be like asking a very cranky boss for time off to help your distant family members rebuild their homes after they burned to the ground in a fire. Instead of your boss saying no, he says yes and gives you the time off with pay. What's more, he actually pays for your trip, pays for the rebuilding of the homes, and buys you a condo to live in while the project is being completed. Now, that's amazing grace!

I like the way Nehemiah described it. He said, "The king granted these requests, because the gracious hand of God was on me" (Neh. 2:8, NLT). We know from reading the story that purpose was also involved. God had selected Nehemiah for this task and wired him with the gifts and talents to accomplish it. Therefore, Nehemiah was positioned to receive grace for the purpose of helping God's people.

Now, I can't tell you the purpose God has in mind for everyone who goes to the next level. However, I can say that if you're willing to position your life to fulfill the purpose of God, grace can't help but find you. It is yours for the asking.

Next-Level Concepts

Grace is not luck. Grace is power that's under the full control of God and is totally dependent on His will. Nothing is left to chance.

GRACE COMES THROUGH PARTNERSHIP

Grace also comes to us by partnering with people who have grace at work in their lives. The apostle Paul is a perfect example. In his letter to the Philippian church, he said their partnership of love, prayer, and financial support qualified them to be *partakers* of his grace. (See Philippians 1:2–7, AMP.) To *partake* means to "share in." This means that those who partnered with Paul could share in the grace that was on his life.

Interestingly, Paul personalizes the grace on his life, calling it "my grace" in many Bible versions. Was he being arrogant? I don't think so. Paul was simply saying that God empowered him with special grace to preach the gospel despite the opposition amassed against him. And those who partnered with him had access to the same type of grace. If they followed his example and partnered with his ministry, they could get the same kind of results in their lives. This is why he was able to confidently tell the Philippians:

> *Being confident of this very thing, that he which hath begun a good work in you will perform it until the day of Jesus Christ.*
>
> —PHILIPPIANS 1:6, KJV

He was confident in this statement because God had graced him to complete his assignments, and therefore He would grace them in their assignments.

Grace through partnership was also evident in the lives of Abraham and his nephew Lot. As we learned earlier, God told Abraham, "Leave your country, your relatives and your father's house, and go the land I will show you" (Gen. 12:1, NLT). In return, God promised to bless Abraham with wealth, power, and generations of offspring. Interestingly, nowhere in the encounter does God mention Lot. Yet when Abraham obeys, he brings Lot along for the ride.

Now, Lot was not a freeloader. He was a real partner. He shared in Abraham's triumphs and troubles. He dug wells and shepherded his sheep right beside him. He shared in all the responsibility, and by default, he shared in all the rewards. One of those rewards was an increase in their livestock. In fact, the Bible says at one point that Abraham and Lot had so many cattle that the land couldn't sustain them living near each other. The blessings God promised Abraham were literally spilling over into Lot's life.

"Well, that's just a Bible story," some might say. "Those kinds of things don't happen in today's world." The truth is, they do. Think about it. Did Dr. Oz start his own show based on his favor alone, or did he leverage the favor that was on Oprah Winfrey? Likewise, did Jennifer Hudson use her own favor to secure notoriety among potential fans, or did she leverage the favor on the *American Idol* brand and Clive Davis to show the world her potential? In both cases, I believe they benefited from those they partnered with.

Next-Level Concepts

Grace comes to you by partnering with
people who have grace at work in their lives.
As you labor side by side with those God is
blessing, blessings pour into your life.

GRACE COMES THROUGH HUMILITY

There is another way you can position yourself to receive God's grace, and it is probably the most important. It is having an attitude of humility. Yes, I said humility. Cultivating a humble heart that is free of pride is the fertile ground needed for God's grace to grow. The Bible says that God "resists the proud, but gives grace to the humble" (James 4:6, NKJV).

If we will humble ourselves and ask God for His grace in every situation we face, He will gladly give it. His supply is endless. Surprisingly, to be humble does not mean you allow others to take advantage of you or that you become a welcome mat for people to walk on. It also doesn't mean you give up or give in when confronted with opposition. Being humble is something completely different. It's about obedience.

In the Book of Exodus, God provides us with a definition of the word *humility* through the life of Pharaoh, the king of Egypt. When Pharaoh was holding the children of Israel captive as slaves, God sent a man named Moses and his brother Aaron to instruct Pharaoh to let them go. Unfortunately, Pharaoh repeatedly refused. Check out one of the accounts:

> *So Moses and Aaron went to Pharaoh and said to*
> *him, "This is what the Lord, the God of the Hebrews,*
> *says: 'How long will you refuse to humble yourself*
> *before me? Let my people go, so that they may*
> *worship me.'"*
>
> —Exodus 10:3, emphasis added

Notice that Pharaoh *refused to do what God commanded him*, and God described it as him refusing to *humble* himself. Thus, the definition of being humble is to simply do what God is telling us to do despite how difficult it may feel. It means to come under, or submit to, God's Word and will for our lives. Therefore, whenever a person chooses to do God's will instead of their will, they qualify for grace.

Next-Level Concepts

Cultivating a humble heart that's free of pride is the fertile ground needed for God's grace to grow. Being humble is doing what God tells you. It means to come under, or submit to, God's Word and will for your life.

I can personally testify to this fact. I remember when I was in college and the Lord told me to end a dating relationship with someone I loved. Needless to say, I didn't want to do it. I didn't want to submit and come under His word of correction. It seemed hard and virtually impossible. However, the moment I humbled myself and did what God asked me to do, I became qualified to walk in the grace I have today. That grace came in the form of the woman I've been happily married to for over nineteen years. If I had only known then what grace was trying to send my way, I wouldn't have struggled with the decision to obey God as long as I did. Trust me. Grace received is always better than grace denied.

Don't Frustrate Yourself

The point I'm trying to make is that life is difficult when you live apart from the grace of God. In fact, it's a struggle. Whenever grace is absent, struggle is present. Whether it's a job you can't perform, a business that won't grow, or a spouse who won't cooperate, you're just running into brick walls without grace. This is why the apostle Paul said he never left home without it. I like the way Webster's Bible Translation describes what Paul said: "I do not frustrate the grace of God" (Gal. 2:21, WBT).

Why frustrate the only person who has the power to help us reach our goal? Why make it difficult for God to work with us? We may not do it intentionally. However, whenever we choose our way instead of God's way, we frustrate His grace and disqualify ourselves from receiving His help. The actual Greek word Paul used was *atheteō*. It means "to nullify, set aside, reject or make void." The last time I checked, the only thing you set aside or reject are things that have little or no value. No wonder grace is frustrated.

Next-Level Concepts

Whenever grace is absent, struggle is present.

I encourage you to humble yourself before God and do what He says. Don't put it off. To disobey will only delay your advancement. I also encourage you to pursue activities where the grace of God is evident. Stop chasing things that clearly aren't working for you. If God is in it, you'll know it. If He isn't, then you'll know that too.

Finally, look for those around you who have God's grace operating in their lives and partner with them. The grace on them will be made available to you. Through grace, the impossible becomes possible. Though it is invisible, it is invincible. It's the indispensable power you need to take you to the next level.

NEXT-LEVEL ACTION STEPS

1. In what specific ways can you see God's grace working in your life? Where do you feel you need more grace?

_____

_____

_____

_____

2. The combination of gifting, focused practice, and grace create a perfect storm of results. Of the three, which would you say you need more of? How can you obtain it?

_____

_____

_____

_____

3. Name at least two people or organizations that have a level of grace on them you would like to see operating in your life. Look for people and organizations who have similar goals and values that are on a higher level than you are. How can you partner with them?

_____

_____

_____

_____

4. Refusing to do what God tells us to do closes the door to His grace. Is there anything God has asked you to do that you have knowingly or unknowingly left undone?

_____

_____

_____

Activity for Advancement: Humility is the fertile ground needed for God's grace to grow. Pride, the opposite of humility, is a major obstacle to receiving grace. Interestingly, pride is easy to spot in the lives of others but often hard to see in ourselves. Take a few moments to pray and ask God to show you any areas in your life where pride is operating. Ask Him to forgive you of anything He reveals and give you the grace to walk in humility.

Scriptures for Meditation: 1 Corinthians 15:10; 2 Corinthians 12:9; Ephesians 4:7; 1 Peter 5:5

TO REACH THE NEXT LEVEL, A REPRESENTATIVE FROM THE LEVEL YOU SEEK MUST SHOW YOU THE WAY

MIKE TOMLIN, HEAD coach of the Pittsburgh Steelers, is no stranger to breaking barriers and reaching new levels of achievement. He's the youngest head coach to ever win a Super Bowl and the third-youngest head coach of any of the four major professional sports programs.

Yet Tomlin will be the first to tell you that no one gets to the next level without help from someone who's been where you want to go. For Tomlin, that help came in the form of two people—John Kruger and Tony Dungy. Both men are former head coaches and Super Bowl winners. Their counsel and wisdom not only provided a path for Tomlin to follow but also gave him the confidence to blaze his own trail. Such are the benefits of having the right people in your life.[19]

THREE TYPES OF PEOPLE YOU'LL MEET

In general, I have found that there are three types of people who will affect your ability to do better than ever: those who benefit from your purpose, those who oppose your purpose, and those who help you fulfill your purpose. I call the first group "the attracted." For Jesus, this group was the masses that followed His ministry. They were the ones who received His healing, ate His fish-and-loaves dinner, and received His forgiveness. "The attracted" are the ones who sing your praises and benefit from what God is doing in your life. They're attracted to the grace that's on you.

For Mike Tomlin, this group is the team's fan base. For a politician, "the attracted" is his constituency. For the business person, it's his customers. For a pastor, it's his congregation. In every arena, it is this important group that helps to define our success. However, their loyalty is not really to us. They follow us because of the benefits they receive. While serving them is important, depending on them is a mistake. This is why Jesus didn't rely on them to fulfill His mission. He understood that the attracted will crown you king one day but crucify you the next. He was sent to the attracted, but He could not be depend on them or entrust Himself to them. (See John 2:23–25.)

Next-Level Concepts

Those who benefit from your purpose are "the attracted." They sing your praises and benefit from what God is doing in your life. Serve them, but don't depend on them.

The next group is called "the assigned." These are the people who constantly fight against what God wants to do in your life. Oftentimes they feel threatened by your potential success and therefore make it their personal assignment to discredit you. The assigned are the ones you wish would just go away. However, they are just as vital as the people who are singing your praises. Why? Because they build your resolve to trust God. When someone from this group is around, there's no time for slacking. You must stay lean, alert, and attentive. For Jesus, these were the religious leaders of His day. For you and me, it is anyone who is trying to stop us from achieving the level God has called us to.

Finally, there are people God specifically sends into your life to help you fulfill your purpose. They can be categorized in two groups: partners and mentors. Partners support you in fulfilling your purpose. They're not casual observers; they're committed warriors who will fight beside you in both good and bad times. A good partner will never leave you to fight alone. They're not in it for personal gain.

Mentors are people who are qualified to help you achieve, perform, and live on levels you never thought were possible. In fact, whenever God wants to bring you to a new level, He will always send a mentor from that level to help you get there. I call these representatives "the attached" because they are tied to your success. For example, when God wanted to launch Elisha into a prophetic ministry, He sent a senior prophet by the name of Elijah to help him. Elisha and Elijah were attached in purpose. Similarly, when God wanted to use Timothy to teach the Jews and Gentiles about Jesus, He sent him one of the greatest teachers in the New Testament—the apostle Paul. Paul and Timothy were attached in purpose. In case after case, God used someone at a higher level to reach down and help someone at a lower level come up. He used a mentor.

Next-Level Concepts

Those who try to oppose your purpose are "the assigned." They are important because they help build your resolve to trust God.

MENTORS TAKE YOU WHERE YOU CAN'T TAKE YOURSELF

By definition, a mentor is a trusted teacher or coach who helps you reach your full potential. Bill McCartney, the legendary coach at the University of Colorado, described the job of mentoring as "taking a player where he can't take himself."[20] Mentors take people to levels they could never reach on their own. Research confirms this to be true. In the world of business, studies show that executives who use a mentor early in their career not only earn more money but also are happier and more satisfied with their careers. Similarly, the NBA uses a mentorship program within its development league (D-League) to help less-experienced athletes reach professional status.

In many cases, the mentee surpasses the success level of the mentor. For example, Elisha did twice as many miracles as Elijah. Gamaliel taught Old Testament law, but Paul, his protégé, taught New Testament grace. Moses led Israel out of Egypt. However, Joshua, his mentee, led Israel into the Promised Land. John the Baptist baptized with water, but Jesus baptized with the Holy Spirit. And while Jesus did many mighty works, He promised that we, His disciples or mentees, would do even greater works.

Next-Level Concepts

Mentors take us where we can't take ourselves. They help us reach levels we could never reach on our own.

MENTORS PROVIDE A CLEAR PATTERN

In general, mentors perform at least two major roles in your life. First and foremost, they provide a pattern or path for you to follow. In her book *The Mentor's Guide: Facilitating Effective Learning Relationships*, author Lois Zachary uses ecology to illustrate the power of having someone or something to follow. She states:

> *A tree planted in a clearing of an old forest will*
> *grow more successfully than one planted in an open*
> *field. The reason, it seems, is that the roots of the*
> *forest tree are able to follow the intricate pathways*
> *created by former trees and thus embed themselves*
> *more deeply. Similarly, human beings thrive best*
> *when we grow in the presence of those who have*
> *gone before.*[21]

This is why Jesus instructed His disciples to follow Him. He was simply saying that we'll grow deeper in our relationship with God by following His example than if we try to blaze our own unproven trail toward what we think is the will of God.

So, here's the ten thousand dollar question: who are the attracted, assigned, and attached in your life? Who are your partners, and who are your mentors?

A mentor is a true friend who provides a pattern for you to imitate. He's not a partner; you're not equal. Instead, he's an elder (not by reason of his age but by reason of his experience) to whom you have given permission to speak into your life. Their words have weight, and their life experience is worth imitating. Consider what the apostle Paul told Timothy:

> *Imitate those who through faith and patience inherit*
> *what has been promised.*
>
> —HEBREWS 6:12

On another occasion Paul encouraged Timothy to follow the pattern of the sound words he had heard from him—in the faith and love that are in Christ Jesus. (See 2 Timothy 1:13.) Paul was encouraging Timothy to use him as a pattern for building his own life. By doing so, Timothy would produce a deeper, fuller life than the one he could produce on his own.

In order to follow this pattern, Timothy would have to spend time observing Paul's life. This is why Paul said:

*Remember your leaders, who spoke the word of God
to you. Consider the outcome of their way of life and
imitate their faith.*

—HEBREWS 13:7

The word *consider* here means "to observe accurately and survey from the lowest to the highest." In other words, the way you follow a mentor is not just by listening but also by observing. What is their attitude like in the face of adversity? What type of work ethic do they have? What do they read? What do they avoid? What are their priorities? How do they handle people? You are not observing to catch them in an error. You are simply searching for proven pathways you can imitate and follow.

Next-Level Concepts

A mentor is a true friend who provides a pattern
for you to imitate. The way you follow a mentor
is not just by listening but also by observing.

Let me give you a quick example. Moses was the mentor of a talented young man named Joshua who had a call of God on his life. Not only was Joshua a man of faith who believed God, but he was also a worshiper. Yet even with these great qualities, there was still something Joshua needed to effectively reach his next level of leadership. I'm not saying faith and worship are unimportant. They are vital. The Bible says that without faith it is impossible to please God, and He looks for those who will worship Him in spirit and truth (Heb. 11:6; John 4:23). Joshua had these attributes. What he needed was a sacrificial love for God's people; he needed a shepherd's heart.

Faith could take Joshua into the Promised Land, but only a shepherd's heart would ensure that others would be able to join him. Joshua's worship could attract the presence of

God, but only a shepherd's heart would desire that everyone experience it. Therefore, God gave Joshua an illustration of the type of heart he needed to reach his next level. Moses was that illustration. By observing how Moses handled God's people in countless situations, Joshua learned how he should handle God's people. Moses's life became a proven pathway for him to follow and imitate. In some cases, it even served as an example of what *not* to do.

Next-Level Concepts

When God wants to bring you to a new level, He always sends someone into your life from the level you seek. Their life becomes a pattern for you to follow.

Mentors Help You Avoid Costly Mistakes

The second major benefit of a mentor is that they help you avoid costly mistakes that could delay or derail your progress to the next level. Think of them as a type of protection for your life. Nowhere is this more evident than in a parent-child relationship. As parents, we not only want our children to walk in their God-given potential, but we also want them to avoid the pitfalls that made our lives difficult. Hence, parents should be their children's first mentors. Consider some of the things Solomon told his son:

> Listen, my son, to your father's instruction and do not forsake your mother's teaching.
> —Proverbs 1:8

> My son, do not forget my teaching, but keep my commands in your heart.
> —Proverbs 3:1

*My son, pay attention to my wisdom, listen well to
my words of insight.*

—Proverbs 5:1

In each instruction Solomon was trying to help his son
avoid costly mistakes that could derail or significantly delay
his progress to the next level. He was protecting his son.
Mentors offer you and me the same protection through their
words of wisdom.

Think about Moses's father-in-law, Jethro. He advised
Moses to delegate some of the responsibility of governing
Israel to a group of capable, God-fearing men. Before Moses
heeded Jethro's advice, he spent the entire day judging the
disputes of hundreds of people. Not only was his health in
jeopardy, but so was the effectiveness of his leadership. Jethro
advised him to appoint leaders to judge small issues among
the people, leaving the more difficult cases to Moses. This
advice would save not only Moses's life but also his ministry.

Prior to Jethro's arrival, Moses was on a collision course
with disaster. Yes, he could call down plagues on Egypt, part
the Red Sea, and make water gush out of a rock. But in spite
of all his anointing and privilege, he still needed a mentor.
He still needed someone to help prevent him from pursuing
a course that was hostile to his future. The same is true for
us. Everyone needs a mentor in their life to help steer them
in the right direction.

Next-Level Concepts

A mentor helps you avoid costly mistakes that
could delay or derail your progress to the
next level. They protect and prevent you from
pursuing a course that is hostile to your future.

The question is, are we willing to listen? Are we willing to confront what our mentors see as our weakness? For example, if your coach says you're not ready to start in the game, do you listen or quit? If your pastor says you need more time before he will ordain you in the ministry, do you wait or find someone else to confirm you? If your parents advise you against marrying the person you're dating, do you become angry or take time to really investigate their concerns? Remember, mentors aren't in your life to make it difficult. They're there to protect you.

Too bad Solomon's son Rehoboam didn't realize this fact. While Solomon was the wisest man in the world, Rehoboam was not so wise. After Solomon's death, the citizens of the land came to their new king Rehoboam and asked for reform in the kingdom. The existing economic and social policies created under King Solomon had served the kingdom well during its formative years. However, as the kingdom matured, the rigid policies became taxing on the people. As a result, the people wanted reform. They said:

> Your father made life hard for us—worked our fingers to the bone. Give us a break; lighten up on us and we'll willingly serve you.
>
> —1 Kings 12:4, The Message

Now, God had given Rehoboam mentors to help him in his weakness and assist him in achieving the call on his life. However, there was also another group of people speaking into his life. Consequently Rehoboam asked for counsel from both groups when trying to decide how to respond to the request of the Israelites. See if you can identify each one according to the categories we identified earlier. The first group gave the following advice:

These people who complain, "Your father was too hard on us; lighten up"—well, tell them this: "My little finger is thicker than my father's waist. If you think life under my father was hard, you haven't seen the half of it. My father thrashed you with whips; I'll beat you bloody with chains!"

—1 KINGS 12:10–11, THE MESSAGE

The second group told Rehoboam:

If you will be a servant to this people, be considerate of their needs and respond with compassion, work things out with them, they'll end up doing anything for you.

—1 KINGS 12:7, THE MESSAGE

Have you figured it out? The first group was "the attracted." These were friends Rehoboam allowed to speak into his life, but they didn't have his best interest in mind. They only saw his position, fame, and power as a means to better their own lives. Hence, they spoke out of their desire, not his need.

The second group was "the attached." More specifically, they were Rehoboam's mentors. These were the elder counselors who had advised Solomon and recognized Rehoboam's need. They saw a young, gifted king but one who also needed to mature in his leadership. Rehoboam needed to learn that leadership is a two-sided coin. One side is authority and power; the other is mercy and compassion. One side is gifting, and the other is character. Rehoboam clearly had one side intact. However, the other side was woefully lacking. His God-given mentors tried to protect him in this vulnerable area of need and, by doing so, highlighted a major distinction between the two groups: people may recognize your gifting, but true mentors recognize your need. Rehoboam's friends basically ranted, "Tell them you're the king! You're the one ordained with power! Forget what your subjects need and want." A true mentor would never advise such actions. A mentor would protect their mentee from such a destructive path.

Next-Level Concepts

People may recognize your gifting, but true mentors recognize your need and seek to help you and protect you from areas of vulnerability.

The prophet Samuel attempted to provide the same type of protection to King Saul. Samuel knew that Saul was gifted and anointed. However, he also recognized Saul's need. He knew that unless Saul could learn "obedience is better than sacrifice" (1 Sam. 15:22), he would never reach his full potential. Therefore, Samuel spent the bulk of his time counseling Saul on issues of obedience, not governmental rule.

Sadly, Saul never learned the lesson and cut his life and kingly rule short. Rehoboam did the same. He failed to heed the counsel of his mentors and nearly lost everything his father worked so hard to achieve. Both kings could have avoided their hardships if they would have simply humbled themselves and accepted the mentors God had sent to help and protect them. Take their examples to heart so that you can avoid the pain they experienced.

WHERE CAN YOU FIND A NEXT-LEVEL MENTOR?

Hopefully I've demonstrated the importance of having a mentor in order to reach your next level. The next question we need to answer is how to find one. Fortunately, mentors are in more places than you can imagine. For example, mentors can be found in your *workplace*. I remember inviting the national sales manager of the company where I worked to lunch one afternoon. I wanted to learn what traits he felt were important to being a good salesman. That meeting ultimately opened the door for me to enter into sales.

Another place mentors are found is at *church*. For example, your pastor should serve as your mentor simply through the example of his life. When I think about the men and women of God who have served as teachers and mentors in my own life, I can definitely attribute my success to their counsel. My first pastors, Clinton and Sarah Utterbach, taught me the importance of excellence and showed me how to honor the presence of God. My current pastor, Dr. Dimitri Bradley, has modeled integrity before me and demonstrated how I should treat people. Finally, John Bevere showed me how to live with passion for God. All of these people were invaluable to my development.

Of course, not everyone you ask will be willing to help in your development. The truth is, finding a mentor is like finding a spouse. Just because you're attracted to someone doesn't mean they want to spend the rest of their life with you. It's the same with a mentor. The mentee has to be willing to seek, and the mentor has to be willing to be found. In other words, mentors don't just show up because you need one. They show up because of what they hear about you and see in you.

The national sales manager was willing to meet with me because of what he had seen and heard about me in the department. This is the same reason Paul met Timothy. The Bible says when Paul came to Derbe, he wasn't coming to find a mentee. That was the last thing on his mind. Yet when the brothers at Lystra and Iconium spoke well of Timothy, Paul took notice. (See Acts 16:1–3.) He heard about Timothy from multiple sources. And it was what he heard that caused him to inquire more. I'm not sure how many men spoke well of Timothy, but it was enough to get Paul's attention.

Here's the point: *mentors are drawn to our lives when others begin to testify about who we are and what we can do.* For instance, King Saul asked David to live in the palace after his servants testified about David's musical abilities (1 Sam. 16:14–23). Similarly, it was the cupbearer's testimony of Joseph's ability to interpret dreams that brought him out of prison and before Pharaoh (Gen. 41:1–14). The same pattern occurred with Paul; it was the testimony of Barnabas that opened the door for Paul to meet Peter (Gal. 2:9).

Therefore, the phrase "looking for a mentor" is somewhat misleading. Yes, we need to openly seek mentors who will give godly guidance and help us make it to the next level. However, mentors will not come to us just because we want to be around them. Mentors will come because of what they see in us and their desire to be involved in our lives.

Next-Level Concepts

Mentors don't just show up because you need one. They show up because of what they hear about you and see in you. They're drawn to you when others begin to testify about you.

ARE YOU *READY* FOR A NEXT-LEVEL MENTOR?

It's easy to say, "I want someone to help me do better." However, are you prepared to handle the rigors of the next level and what a mentor might expect of you? For example, the apostle Paul and Barnabas took a young man by the name of John Mark as their mentee during their first missionary journey. After several nights of hardship, confrontations with demons, and outright persecutions, John Mark began wondering what he had gotten himself into. By the time they were ready to leave for Pamphylia, the Bible says John Mark deserted Paul and Barnabas and returned to Jerusalem. (See Acts 15:37–38.) He had had enough. He wanted the next level, but the process required to get there was more than he was able to handle at the time.

When you examine what happened on the surface, it's hard to empathize with John Mark. Why would anyone who wanted to do great things for God abandon the opportunity to learn from such an anointed man? Paul seemed like a mentee's dream. He was so anointed by God that demons knew his name. He operated in the gifts of healing, tongues, interpretation of tongues, faith, the word of wisdom, and the word of knowledge. He was even used by God to write two-thirds of the New Testament! He was caught up into heaven and received revelations from God that were so incredible that God prohibited him from sharing some of them. Who wouldn't want to be mentored by such a spiritual giant?

What many people forget, however, is that Paul was also whipped with thirty-nine lashes five different times. He was beaten with rods, imprisoned, and suffered starvation for his faith. He was robbed, chased as a fugitive, and betrayed by people he trusted. He was denied the comfort of marriage and went without sleep on many occasions. He was shipwrecked three times and even stoned to death and brought back to life. Is it any wonder he despaired of life at times and at one point described his existence as "a sentence of death" (2 Cor. 1:9)? Yet through it all, God's grace was sufficient for Paul. It was strong enough to lift him out of whatever pit he encountered.

For John Mark, on the other hand, the reality and application of God's grace was not fully understood. When he first left on the missionary journey, he was brimming with excitement. However, when the reality of what he had undertaken finally began to sink in, his view changed.

Isn't it funny how different things can look up close than

from a distance? From afar, things can appear great. However, when we examine them up close, we get a whole new perspective. The same is true with mentoring. From a distance, next-level mentors appear to be perfect and live perfect lives, but that is not the case. We see everything in them that we want for our lives. We want to perform and operate on their level. We want the notoriety they have and long for the power they possess and flow in. Yet in our pursuit, we often overlook the cost required to live at their level.

This is why Jesus asked two of His mentees, James and John, who wanted to operate on His level, "Are you really prepared to drink of My cup?" (See Mark 10:37–39.) In other words, "Are you ready to take on the responsibility and sacrifice required to live at this level?" He was telling them—and us—that mentorship has two inseparable sides: authority and responsibility. We can't walk in the power of our mentor's gifting and not share in the burden (cup of responsibility and sacrifice) of his calling.

You can't say, "I want to play basketball like Kobe Bryant," and not share his rigorous and demanding work ethic. You can't say, "I want to have an international ministry like John Bevere," and not be willing to leave your family for many days on end. When you are ready to accept the responsibility and sacrifices of the next level, you are truly ready for a next-level mentor. And when you are ready, a mentor will come to you. Perhaps this is what the Africans mean when they say, "When a student is ready, a teacher will come."

Next-Level Concepts

When you're ready to accept the responsibility and sacrifices of the next level, you're truly ready for a next-level mentor. And when you're ready, a mentor will come to you.

WHAT DOES IT MEAN TO BE READY?

When you're ready, it means you're *committed*. It means you're willing to leave what you've known so you can experience what you've dreamed. Let me give you an example. Elisha was selected by God to become the next great prophet of Israel. However, he knew very little about being a prophet. His livelihood was farming. So what did God do when He wanted to take a man from one level (farming) to another level (prophesying)? He sent a representative from the higher level to help him get there. In this case, the representative was Elijah.

When the prophet Elijah arrived at Elisha's home, the Bible says he simply threw his cloak on Elisha and left (1 Kings 19:19). There's no record of Elijah speaking a prophetic word or praying a long prayer. You don't hear the prophet say, "I believe God wants to use you, Elisha." Nothing like that happens. All we see is a dusty garment thrown on a man who is plowing his field. Yet Elisha knew what it meant. It was an invitation to go to the next level.

All Elisha had to do to enter it was commit to follow the man who was already there. However, listen to the way Elisha responded: "Please let me kiss my father and my mother, and then I will follow you" (1 Kings 19:20, NKJV). The request seemed reasonable. It was his father's field he was plowing. He couldn't just leave without saying good-bye—his parents would be worried sick. Yet the prophet's response was as cold as ice: "Go back again, for what have I done to you?" Translation: Forget it. You aren't ready for me.

How rude! Couldn't Elijah at least let Elisha tell his folks he was leaving? It wasn't that he didn't want to go to the next level. It's just that the call came at an inconvenient time. He was right in the middle of plowing a huge field for his parents. If he simply left, what would happen to the twelve oxen he was using? Couldn't the prophet at least wait until Elisha put away the animals? Of course he could. However, I believe God was highlighting an important truth: when He sends someone into your life to help you reach a new level, your intentions don't define your readiness—your actions do.

Next-Level Concepts

When God sends someone into your life to help you reach a new level, your intentions don't define your readiness—your actions do.

Now let's contrast Elisha's response to God's call with the response of the disciples when their mentor, Jesus, called them. Scripture says:

> *As Jesus was walking beside the Sea of Galilee, he saw two brothers, Simon called Peter and his brother Andrew. They were casting a net into the lake, for they were fishermen. "Come, follow me," Jesus said, "and I will make you fishers of men." At once they left their nets and followed him.*
>
> *Going on from there, he saw two other brothers, James son of Zebedee and his brother John. They were in a boat with their father Zebedee, preparing their nets. Jesus called them, and immediately they left the boat and their father and followed him.*
> —MATTHEW 4:18–22, EMPHASIS ADDED

What a difference! The disciples left their boats, equipment, and crew "at once" and "immediately" to follow Jesus after He said, "Follow Me." Peter responded so quickly that he literally left his nets in the water! Matthew responded just as quickly and emphatically. The Bible says that when Jesus asked the infamous tax collector to follow Him, Matthew got up *immediately* and left his booth containing the taxes he had been collecting. He must have really wanted to go to a new level in God to purposely leave a booth full of money!

Were these men crazed lunatics, chasing after a radical preacher? Or were they chasing after something more than just flesh and blood? I believe they were chasing after something more. They were desperate for a higher level of living, and when they ran into a Man who was clearly living where they wanted to go, they didn't skip a beat chasing after Him. They were ready to learn from Him, serve Him, and grow from His wisdom. How do we know they were ready? Because of their actions—not their words or their intentions. They were totally committed to Christ, and it showed in what they did.

Unfortunately, not all of the disciples Jesus called were ready for the level they claimed they wanted. One disciple was asked to follow Jesus, but he couldn't do it because it would have affected his finances. (See Matthew 19:21–22.) In another case, the would-be disciple wanted to go bury his relatives first. Jesus said to him, "Let the dead bury their own dead" (Luke 9:60). Now, that's rough! I thought Elijah was cold, but Jesus made Elijah look like Mother Teresa. This man simply wanted to bury his mama, and he couldn't. Where's the compassion? Where's the sympathy?

Again, I believe God is emphasizing an important point. He's not saying you have to so blindly follow mentors and teachers that you become reckless and irresponsible to your family and other commitments. That is not the way God works. His order of priority is always God first, then family, then service to others.

Next-Level Concepts

When God wants to bring you to a new level,
He will always send you a representative
from that level to help you get there.

In these examples, I believe He is emphasizing a very important next-level law: when God wants to bring you to a new level, He will always send you someone on that level to help you get there. Your ability to be received by that person and enter their level will not be determined by what you say or your intentions. Your actions will determine your readiness for the next level. What you do when they arrive in your life and invite you into fellowship will tell the true preparedness of your heart. Are you totally committed? Are you willing to leave what you've known so you can experience what you've dreamed? Are you ready to move forward and be mentored by the representative God wants to send your way? If you're ready, then take the action steps listed on the next page.

NEXT-LEVEL ACTION STEPS

1. Take a moment and identify people in your life who fall into each of these groups.

The Attracted	The Assigned	The Attached
_____	_____	_____
_____	_____	_____
_____	_____	_____

2. "The attached" are those who are tied to your success. They are the mentors God has placed in your life. Are you open and receptive to their direction? What are the dangers of being closed? What are the advantages of being open?

_____

_____

_____

_____

_____

3. Stop and take an honest look at yourself. What areas in your character would you say are the most vulnerable? How can you strengthen them? Pray and ask God for His input.

_____

_____

_____

_____

4. What is your most desired "next-level" experience? What are some of the responsibilities and sacrifices required of this next level? Are you ready to accept them?

_____

_____

_____

_____

_____

Activity for Advancement: Identify two people who operate at a higher level of success than you in the four areas below. Make an appointment to take one person in each group to lunch over the course of the next six weeks. Discover what they read, their priorities, their beliefs, and their disciplines, and write them in the spaces below.

Area	Person 1	Priorities, Disciplines, Beliefs, and What They Read	Person 2	Priorities, Disciplines, Beliefs, and What They Read
Relationship w/God				
Marriage				
Job/Business				
Fitness/ Health				

From your discussion with each person and your personal readings, identify and jot down specific steps you can take to improve your life in all of the areas listed below.

Area	Specific Steps I Can Take to Improve My Life in These Areas
Relationship w/ God	
Marriage	

Area	Specific Steps I Can Take to Improve My Life in These Areas
Job/Business	
Fitness/Health	

Scriptures for Meditation: Psalm 75:6–7; 111:10; Proverbs 1:7; 9:10; 14:27; 16:20; 19:23; 22:4; 23:11

YOUR LEVEL OF PREPARATION WILL DETERMINE YOUR LEVEL OF HARVEST

I F YOU WERE to drive down the street in your neighborhood and see a surveyor measuring the property line of a vacant lot, what would you think? Most likely you would think that a new home is about to be built. Even though bulldozers aren't digging up the ground and framers aren't nailing together two-by-fours, the mere fact that a surveyor is defining a property line suggests that preparation is being made for something new that is about to happen.

Similarly, if you came home late one evening and walked in the house, only to find the kids gone, soft music playing, and a trail of scented rose petals leading upstairs to your bedroom, it wouldn't take a rocket scientist to know that your spouse is preparing for something special to happen. Scented rose petals and romantic music are not the types of preparation one would make if they were planning to fix a leaky faucet or file their taxes. These are preparations that stir up greater expectations. In both of these examples, the level and type of preparation a person makes gives a clue about the type of harvest they expect to receive.

Next-Level Concepts

The level and type of preparation you make gives a clue about the type of harvest you expect to receive.

THE VALUE OF THE HARVEST IS
REFLECTED IN THE PREPARATION

In general, your level of preparation not only forecasts the type of harvest you expect to receive, but it also communicates how valuable your harvest is to you. Let me give you a sad but true example from my own life to explain.

A few years ago, my twelve-year-old daughter joined her school's band as a piano player. Each year the school holds an annual recital, and for the first time my daughter had the opportunity to participate. For weeks she had been telling us about the event to ensure we would all be there on time. Many of her friends were in the band, and she didn't want to miss it—especially since her group was only doing one song. The recital started at 6:00 p.m. This meant we had to pick her up from school at 3:30 p.m., rush home to eat, and be back to the school before her group went on stage. Unfortunately, by the time we arrived home, it was already 4:30 p.m., and we hadn't prepared any dinner. Frantically, we agreed on the right outfit, fixed unruly hair, and threw together some food. By then it was 5:30 p.m. We had exactly thirty minutes to get to her school that was at least forty-five minutes away!

Needless to say, we dashed out of the house like crazed parents. By the time we got through traffic, found a parking spot, and ran into the auditorium, we were just in time to see her band finish the one and only song they were scheduled to play. In that moment, my daughter turned and looked at me with an expression I will never forget. I felt like I had swallowed a wad of mud. I was so disappointed. We really wanted to see her perform. However, our lack of preparation communicated an entirely different message to her about what was important to us.

We learned a very valuable lesson that day: *failure to properly prepare and be organized for what we claim is important will delay or jeopardize our ability to receive it.*

Next-Level Concepts

Failure to properly prepare and be
organized for your next level will delay or
jeopardize your ability to receive it.

Jesus taught this principle in a parable He told the disciples. He said:

Then shall the kingdom of heaven be likened unto ten virgins, which took their lamps, and went forth to meet the bridegroom. And five of them were wise, and five were foolish. They that were foolish took their lamps, and took no oil with them: But the wise took oil in their vessels with their lamps. While the bridegroom tarried, they all slumbered and slept. And at midnight there was a cry made, Behold, the bridegroom cometh; go ye out to meet him. Then all those virgins arose, and trimmed their lamps. And the foolish said unto the wise, Give us of your oil; for our lamps are gone out. But the wise answered, saying, Not so; lest there be not enough for us and you: but go ye rather to them that sell, and buy for yourselves. And while they went to buy, the bridegroom came; and they that were ready went in with him to the marriage: and the door was shut. Afterward came also the other virgins, saying, Lord, Lord, open to us. But he answered and said, Verily I say unto you, I know you not.

—MATTHEW 25:1–12, KJV, EMPHASIS ADDED

Notice what distinguished the wise virgins from the foolish: their level of preparation. All ten of them desired a relationship with the bridegroom. However, when we evaluate their desire by their level of preparation, a clear difference emerges between the two groups of women. All ten had lamps so that they could see when the bridegroom came. However, only five made extra preparations to ensure they wouldn't run out of lamp oil should the bridegroom tarry. I believe this parable brings out two important points that are relevant to doing better than ever in life.

Point 1

Time is an enemy for the unprepared. In this parable, the bridegroom came at midnight—the most inconvenient of times to come. Hence, instead of it being an occasion of joy for the women, it was a time of stress for those who were not prepared. If only they had had another hour to go and buy what they needed, everything would have been perfect. But they didn't, and they missed their moment.

Point 2

The time you spend preparing never exceeds the time you waste by being unprepared. In this parable, it looked like the wise virgins lost more time, energy, and money lugging around extra oil. However, their loss was insignificant compared to the loss of the foolish virgins.

Since it was pitch-black outside and their lamps went out, it must have taken the foolish virgins twice as long to find their way back to the market to buy extra oil. Furthermore, seeing that it was midnight, it was very unlikely that anyone would even be awake to sell oil at such an hour. When they finally did find someone willing to get out of bed and sell them oil, the merchant would have probably demanded a premium price. By the time the foolish virgins returned, they had missed out on what they claimed was important to them. They were denied entrance into the promise that could have been theirs to enjoy.

Indeed, the price of being unprepared is very costly. If we really value the harvest ahead, we must adequately invest in the needed preparation. This is what Jesus did. He spent approximately thirty years preparing in private for what would only be three years of public ministry. During this time Jesus wasn't just sitting around waiting for His "appointed time." The Bible says that He "grew in wisdom and favor with God and man." He grew to the point where His current level couldn't hold Him.

At first glance, it appears as if Jesus had little time to benefit from the fruit of His labors. In fact, it almost looks as if His level of preparation did little to affect His level of harvest. Thirty years of preparation versus three years of harvest. On the surface, it doesn't add up. However, upon closer examination, we learn otherwise. Jesus is still enjoying the harvest of His preparation. Those thirty years of praying, studying, listening, and learning have produced approximately two thousand years of harvest for Jesus—and He's still reaping! Every time someone gets saved, every time someone receives healing, every time someone turns from darkness to light, it represents another level of harvest for Jesus.

Next-Level Concepts

Time is an enemy for the unprepared. The time you spend preparing never exceeds the time you waste by being unprepared.

ARE YOU PREPARED FOR YOUR DEFINING MOMENT?

Life-changing opportunities rarely forecast their arrival. They can happen anytime, anywhere, without notice. In an instant and out of nowhere, something so ridiculously awesome can happen that categorically changes the course of your destiny.

The question is, are you ready for it? Are you prepared for your defining moment?

David Foster, the acclaimed songwriter and producer, certainly was. For those of you who may not know David, you certainly will know his work. For almost four decades he has produced more hits than almost any living person on the planet. In the late 1970s, he produced the Grammy Award–winning song "After the Love Has Gone," recorded by Earth, Wind, and Fire. In 1982 he was nominated for Producer of the Year. In 1984 he won another Grammy for his arrangement of "Hard Habit to Break" by Chicago. That same year he wrote the original score for the motion picture *Ghostbusters*. In 1985 he was nominated for Album of the Year for his work on *We Are the World* and Best Pop Instrumental Performance for the "Love Theme From St. Elmo's Fire." And the list goes on and on. Foster has worked with Chaka Khan, Natalie Cole, Whitney Houston, Celine Dion, Madonna, Andrea Bocelli, N'SYNC, and Michael Jackson. It's no wonder they call him the "Hitman."

Yet Foster's success didn't come by accident. It came by appointment. And when it arrived, he was ready for it. For years Foster made his living as a successful musician, playing for the likes of George Harrison, Paul McCartney, and Diana Ross. However, as he explains in his book *Hitman*, he didn't want to grow old in a job that prides itself on replacing old musicians with younger and cheaper talent. Hence, becoming a producer seemed like the logical next-level step. He writes:

> *The first thing that occurred to me was that I had the talent to become a producer. I had worked for dozens of producers, and at times I had even found myself doing the jobs of some of the weaker ones, and I realized that most of them didn't know much about music. I would watch those producers flailing around, and it was clear to me that they survived*

117

by getting the studio musicians, guys like me, to do their jobs for them.[22]

Then one day destiny came calling. His moment of truth had arrived, and it came in the form of a recording session for Barbra Streisand. Foster had been called in along with a few other keyboard players for what would be a full orchestra performance for Streisand's new project. He was placed off in a corner during the session and, for all intents and purposes, was invisible to Barbra. As fate would have it, the session wasn't going well. The arrangement never really struck a chord with Streisand, and she became increasingly frustrated with the producer on the project for his failure to give her the sound she was looking for. After several takes, things went from bad to worse. So much so, they decided to call it quits and break for lunch. Foster explains what happened next:

> *Clearly, I was aware of the scope of the problem, and—ever the opportunist—I didn't go to lunch. I stayed behind nodding at the piano, playing the song the way I thought it should be played, and the way I thought Barbra wanted it played, based on what I'd been able to pick up from her conversations with Rupert (the producer). And suddenly I heard that familiar voice: "Hey you! What is that!? What is that you just played?" she asked. "Can you play it again?"*[23]

It was Barbra Streisand. She had come in at the right moment and heard what Foster was playing, and she loved it. She turned to the producer on the project and said, "Did you hear that? Let's do it like that." That moment defined Foster's future and would ultimately set him on course to become one of the greatest music producers in history. Thank goodness he decided to stay behind and prepare something for her to hear. If he had gone to McDonald's or to check his phone messages, he would have missed his moment.

Next-Level Concepts

Life-changing opportunities rarely forecast their arrival. They can happen anytime, anywhere, without notice. The question is, are you ready for it?

GOD PREPARES, THEN RELEASES

The opportunities that ultimately came to Foster didn't come by chance. There's no such thing as chance or luck when it comes to going to the next level. God's grace opens a door that we can't open on our own and empowers us to do what we could never do in our own strength. He then prepares us for what He has prepared for us. And our level of preparation determines our level of harvest. It's a law. This is why God always prepares before He releases. Think about it. He spent six days preparing the earth before He released Adam and Eve to live in it. Before He released a flood, He had Noah prepare an ark. Prior to sending Jesus, He sent John the Baptist to prepare the way. We see this pattern all throughout Scripture. God prepares, then He releases.

There is a wonderful illustration of this truth in the life of the apostle Peter. When Peter was first called into ministry, his sole focus was to minister to the Jewish people. According to his custom and interpretation of religious law, it was unlawful for him to even go into the home of a Gentile, much less preach to one. Ministering salvation to the Gentiles was unthinkable. Yet that is exactly what God wanted to do. He wanted to release Peter into an entirely new level of ministry. However, He couldn't release him until he was prepared to receive what God wanted to release. So what did God do? He prepared Peter by showing him a very strange vision. While praying on the rooftop one afternoon, Peter fell into a trance. And then:

> *He saw heaven opened and something like a large sheet being let down to earth by its four corners. It contained all kinds of four-footed animals, as well as reptiles of the earth and birds of the air. Then a voice told him, "Get up, Peter. Kill and eat."*
>
> —ACTS 10:11–13

When Peter saw the vision, he immediately said, "No, Lord, I've never eaten unclean things" (v. 14). So God gave him the same vision two more times. I can almost hear Peter thinking to himself, "Why in the world would the Lord ask me to eat something that is unlawful for a Jewish person to eat?" And just as he was thinking about the meaning, a knock came at the door where he was staying. Amazingly, it was a group of Gentile men asking to speak with Peter. They had been sent by a well-regarded Gentile man named Cornelius and were told to ask Peter to come to his house. Under normal circumstances, Peter would have declined. However, having just been given this vision, Peter was open to at least investigate what God might be doing. So off he went with a few trusted friends to back him up if needed.

Next-Level Concepts

God prepares you for what He has prepared
for you. And your level of preparation
determines your level of harvest. It's a law.
God always prepares before He releases.

When Peter arrived at Cornelius's home, what took place was nothing like Peter had expected. There wasn't just one man waiting for Peter. Cornelius had rounded up all his relatives and friends. There were food, drinks, and people everywhere. Peter wasn't just stepping into a Gentile home. He was stepping into a Gentile party!

What on earth had he done? How would he ever explain this to the other disciples? When Cornelius saw Peter, he ran and fell at his feet as if Christ Himself had walked in the door. Peter lifted him up and asked nervously why he had been summoned. Then Cornelius explained that he had had a dream from God. I imagine Peter was probably shocked just to hear that God was speaking to the Gentiles. Nevertheless, Cornelius went on to explain that an angel had asked him to send for Peter so that he could show Cornelius and his family the way of salvation. At this, Peter was stunned. Was it all a coincidence? Could it be that the repeated vision he had had was God's way of preparing him for something new He wanted to release?

As soon as Peter began to open his mouth and explain the same message of salvation he had been preaching to countless Jews, the Bible says the power of God hit Cornelius's house. Everyone in the entire room was filled with God's Spirit! In an instant, the group of Gentiles assembled was catapulted to an entirely new level, and so was Peter's ministry. This was God's intention all along. He wanted to send His power, but He needed a vessel that was prepared to receive it.

I believe God faces the same dilemma today. He wants to release new blessings on a business, but is it fiscally prepared to receive them? He wants to expand the influence of a ministry, but does it have enough integrity to carry it? This is what Jesus was speaking about to His disciples prior to His crucifixion. He wanted to release so much more truth to them, but they weren't ready to receive it. He said:

I have many more things to say to you, but you cannot bear them now.

—JOHN 16:12, NASU

The word *bear* means "to carry, support and uphold." Jesus was telling His disciples and us that our ability to receive new levels of blessing, authority, and power is directly related to our preparation for those levels. This doesn't just apply to revelations from heaven. It applies to every area of life, including the grades we get in school, the positions we hold at work, and the degree of influence and favor we have with others.

Next-Level Concepts

Our ability to receive new levels of blessing, authority, and power is directly related to our preparation for those levels.

I often wonder what would have happened if God had not prepared Peter for his encounter with Cornelius. Would he have accepted the Gentile messengers who knocked at his door? How would he have responded when he saw the party taking place at Cornelius's house? My guess is that Peter would have stayed at the level he was familiar with. He never would have taken such a bold, new step. Consequently, he would have missed out on the new thing God was releasing in the earth.

The same thing will happen to us if we don't remain open to the new things God wants to do in and through our lives. Wise King Solomon summed it up well when he said:

The intelligent man is always open to new ideas. In fact, he looks for them.

—PROVERBS 18:15, TLB

It was God's intention all along to pour out the fresh, new wine of His Spirit upon all flesh—including the Gentiles. It had been prophesied by the prophet Joel centuries earlier. The problem was that Peter was still using old wineskins. He was looking for the manifestation of Christ's New Testament grace but trying to fit it into Old Testament thinking. Thank God for His merciful intervention! Through His great love He prevented Peter from losing out on the new thing He was releasing. He prepared Peter to be a key player in what He was doing. God desires to do the same thing in your life, if you will let Him.

PREPARATION PREVENTS LOSS

Peter's encounter with Cornelius shows that preparation not only helps us receive what God wants to release, but it also helps prevent us from losing the blessing that's been given. Jesus illustrated this principle when He fed the multitudes in the wilderness.

One evening, after teaching countless numbers of people, Jesus instructed His disciples to feed the crowd that had been following Him for several days. This might not have been a problem if it had been just a few people. However, there were more than five thousand men present. If we add in women and children, the number quickly balloons to over ten thousand. Quite bewildered, His disciples asked, "How can we get food to feed so many?" Jesus answered, giving them instructions of preparation:

> *"Make them sit down in groups of fifty." And they did so, and made them all sit down.*
> —LUKE 9:14–15, NKJV

Now, remember, there were more than ten thousand people scattered across an open, grassy field, and there were only twelve disciples! Furthermore, the disciples had just come back from ministering in the neighboring towns, and they were tired and hungry. The last thing they probably wanted to do was organize ten thousand people in groups of fifty and serve them dinner! No matter how you do the math, it equals a lot of work. If each disciple served an equal amount of people, then they would have been responsible for at least sixteen groups!

Didn't Jesus understand this? Why couldn't He just let the people sit down wherever they wanted? Why all the organizing? Why such preparation? Why the focus on order? Well, as we have already stated, God always prepares, and then He releases. Therefore, in order to release what the people needed, which was food, He first had to get them prepared to receive it. Look again at what Jesus did:

> But he said to his disciples, "Have them sit down in groups of about fifty each." The disciples did so, and everybody sat down. Taking the five loaves and the two fish and looking up to heaven, he gave thanks and broke them. Then he gave them to the disciples to set before the people. They all ate and were satisfied.
>
> —LUKE 9:14–17

Only after the people were prepared did the food show up. Equally amazing is what happened after the people were fed. Jesus instructed the disciples to do something else. Scripture says:

> So when they were filled, He said to His disciples, "Gather up the fragments that remain, so that nothing is lost."
>
> —JOHN 6:12, NKJV, EMPHASIS ADDED

Jesus had the disciples prepare the people to receive what God wanted to release. Their preparation also prevented them from losing the fullness of the blessing that was given. Since the multitude was carefully placed in groups of fifty, it was much easier to collect the leftovers from each group. How easy do you think it would have been to try and collect bits and pieces of food from ten thousand individual people scattered across an open plain? Somehow I doubt the disciples would have been able to collect as much. Surely, some of the leftovers would have been lost. However, by preparing the people, Jesus not only increased the efficiency of His ministry, but He also saved time and money.

In all four Gospels, the Bible says the disciples collected twelve baskets of leftovers—one basket for each disciple! (See Matthew 14:20; Mark 6:43; Luke 9:17; John 6:12–13.) This meant they wouldn't have to buy food again for a few days. I believe the same kind of benefit is available to you and me as we cooperate with God's preparation for a next-level release in our lives. Your preparation determines not only the quality of your harvest but also how long you can enjoy it. Through preparation, not one ounce of His blessing will be lost.

NEXT-LEVEL ACTION STEPS

1. Are you prepared for your defining moment—the "big break" you've been looking for? If so, how? If not, how can you prepare?

_____

_____

_____

_____

_____

2. Is God doing something in your life that you don't understand? Pray and ask God to show you how it is preparing you for your God-defining moment.

_____

_____

_____

_____

_____

3. List three next-level goals you want to achieve, and then document at least two preparation steps you think are necessary to achieve them. As always, pray and ask the Lord how He would have you prepare.

Goal 1	
Preparation Step 1	
Preparation Step 2	
Goal 2	
Preparation Step 1	
Preparation Step 2	
Goal 3	
Preparation Step 1	
Preparation Step 2	

Activity for Advancement: Over the course of the next week, journal how you spend your time. How much of it are you using to help you reach your next-level goals? Identify the goal you worked on, the type of preparation you did, and an estimate of the amount of time you invested.

Day of Week	Goal Worked On	Description of Preparation	Time Invested
Monday			
Tuesday			
Wednesday			
Thursday			
Friday			
Saturday			
Sunday			

Scriptures for Meditation: Proverbs 6:6–8; 10:4–5; 12:11; 13:4; 22:29; Luke 12:35–36

YOUR NEXT LEVEL IS
NEVER JUST FOR YOU

E VERYONE WANTS TO reach his or her next level and experience a richer, more fulfilling life. However, the reality is that your next level is never just for you. Yes, each of us wants to expand our business, build a better home, increase our salary, and raise great kids. However, if our only motivation for achieving these goals is merely personal gain, we forfeit the power needed to obtain the very thing we seek. The Bible says it this way:

> You don't have what you want because you don't ask God for it. And even when you ask, you don't get it because your motives are all wrong—you want only what will give you pleasure.
> —JAMES 4:2–3, NLT

In this scripture, God is telling us two things. First, He is saying He has the power to give us the things we desire. Second, He's highly motivated to give things to people who are willing to share what He's given with others. This is the way God works. He blesses us so that we can be a blessing to others. Let me give you a personal testimony to illustrate what I mean.

Next-Level Concepts

Your next level is never just for you. God blesses
us so we can be a blessing to others.

Several years ago I received a substantial raise on my job. It
was the answer to years of prayer, and it meant my wife and I
would be able to furnish and build an addition onto our home.
The increase literally represented another level of prosperity
for my family. However, around the same time, God placed
another family on our hearts who had a significant financial
need concerning their daughter. The timing was amazing. No
sooner had we received the increase and determined how we
were going to spend it, when God showed us a family in great
need. It was as if God was saying, "Not all of the increase I
gave you is for you. I blessed you so that you could also be a
blessing."

Of course, it would have been so easy to say, "God, I need
this money," and then spend it on what our family needed
and wanted. However, I could see what God was trying to do.
He wasn't commanding me to give. He was simply showing
me that this child and her family were important to Him,
and He was blessing me so that I could in turn bless her.

Yes, it would have been nice to add a new screened-in porch
to our house. Yes, we would have loved to buy a few more
pieces of furniture. However, there was a greater need calling
at the time. This is not to say that buying things with the
money God gives us is wrong. I do it all the time. However,
the key to recognizing when God is bringing you to a new
level is first understanding why He's bringing you there. We
truly believed He increased us, in part, to help demonstrate
His faithfulness to others.

Once we gave the money, we received an immediate reward.
No, it wasn't more money. No one walked up to us and gave

us a check. And it wasn't another job. Our immediate reward was *joy*—joy unspeakable and full of glory! We were absolutely elated that we had the chance to partner with God and demonstrate His goodness. Think about it. Our simple act of obedience resulted in an entire family praising God and a little girl experiencing His love and faithfulness. Now that's a reward!

However, God didn't stop there. He took what we gave Him, pressed it down, shook it together, and caused a blessing to begin running over in our lives, so much so that over the course of the next twelve months, the salary I had previously received was increased times four! My new wage put us in an entirely new tax bracket and opened up yet another next-level blessing.

Every time we look back and think about what happened that year, we're amazed. We're also thankful we didn't hoard all that God gave us. I honestly believe we could have built the addition and not given the money. We could have bought the furniture and simply committed the family's need to God in prayer. But would we have experienced the fullness of blessing God intended to give us? Indeed, God's blessings are often disguised as opportunities to help someone else. I believe this is why He brings us to the next level. It's not just for our own personal benefit; it's to demonstrate His goodness.

Next-Level Concepts

God's blessings are often disguised as opportunities to help someone else. They're not just for your own personal benefit; they're to demonstrate His goodness.

YOU ARE BLESSED TO BE A BLESSING!

When God gives you an opportunity to go to the next level, it's not really for you. Yes, you receive benefits, but His focus is beyond you. He always has someone else in mind. Perhaps the best evidence of this fact is how God used the kings of Israel in Old Testament times. When a person was crowned king, he was given total authority in the land. He answered to no one but God. There were no checks and balances to hold him accountable. There was no separation of powers. In fact, there were no other powers. The king was "da man!" No one was higher, and no one had more influence. Even the priests and prophets, who directly reported to God, were submitted to the king. If the king had any common sense, he would listen to the counsel of the prophets and priests. However, he could choose to do as he pleased.

Furthermore, kings were loaded. Financially and materially, they lacked for nothing. Their subjects amply supplied every need and desire they could ever imagine. For example, it's believed that King Solomon received twenty five tons of gold annually. Yes, I said *tons*, not ounces. Solomon also had so much silver that he treated it like the rocks you would find in your backyard. Clearly, it was good to be the king.

All that being said, it must also be noted that when God chose a king, He wasn't trying to make one man blessed and everyone else envious. On the contrary, He was looking for someone He could empower to help the nation live in God's fullness. King David, Solomon's father, was the first king to acknowledge this fact. After he had conquered his enemies, expanded his kingdom, and built a monstrous palace, he realized that everything he had done and obtained was for more than just him. A few years earlier he had been a sheepherder and a fugitive who had virtually nothing. Now he had risen to the top of the greatest empire in the world and was living as king. Foreign nations actually used their national treasuries to help build his palace—a house that made the homes on *MTV Cribs* look like an outhouse.

At that moment, at the zenith of his success, David could have kicked his feet up and declared, "It's great to be king!" But that's not what he did. After God subdued his enemies, placed him on the throne, and blessed him exceedingly, abundantly above and beyond any level he had previously known, David had a revelation. Scripture says:

> *Then King Hiram of Tyre sent messengers to David, along with cedar timber and carpenters and stonemasons, and they built David a palace. And David realized that the Lord had confirmed him as king over Israel and had blessed his kingdom for the sake of his people Israel.*
> —2 SAMUEL 5:11–12, NLT, EMPHASIS ADDED

David recognized he had been given a new level of power, authority, and prosperity—not just for himself but also for the sake of God's great people, Israel. This is what made David different from so many other kings. He realized that God was simply using him as a visual illustration of where He wanted to take His people. David became a channel of blessing to those he served.

This is also the heart of God for you and me. He blesses us so that those around us can also be blessed.

Next-Level Concepts

When God gives you an opportunity to go to the next level, it's not really for you. His focus is beyond you. He always has someone else in mind.

The queen of Sheba recognized this fact when she met King Solomon, David's successor. Although she was pretty loaded herself, her jaw dropped open in awe when she saw all of Solomon's wealth and wisdom. In response to the abundant blessings on his life, she lifted up her voice and said:

> *Everything I heard in my country about your achievements and wisdom is true! I didn't believe what was said until I arrived here and saw it with my own eyes. In fact, I had not heard the half of it! Your wisdom and prosperity are far beyond what I was told.*
>
> —1 KINGS 10:6–7, NLT

Not only did the queen of Sheba recognize the blessing on Solomon's life, but she also recognized that all of his wisdom, power, wealth, and influence were given to him for a reason. She understood that God brings us to another level so we can be a blessing to others. With sincere admiration, she declared:

> *Praise the Lord your God, who delights in you and has placed you on the throne of Israel. Because of the Lord's eternal love for Israel, he has made you king so you can rule with justice and righteousness.*
>
> —1 KINGS 10:9, NLT, EMPHASIS ADDED

Solomon was brought to a new level so that he could be a blessing to God's people. He was blessed to be a blessing. And as a result of the exceedingly, abundantly above next-level blessing flowing through his life, praise was given to God! This kind of reminds me of what Jesus said in Matthew 5:16: "Let your good deeds shine out for all to see, so that everyone will praise your heavenly Father" (NLT).

The New Testament repeatedly confirms that we are blessed to be a blessing. Look at the apostle Paul. He was given the ability to do extraordinary miracles. He was caught up into heaven and received special revelations from God. On one occasion he released the power of God on a man and made him blind that he might see the light of salvation through Christ. Scripture also says that people took garments that touched Paul's body and then placed them on people who were sick, and they were healed—even days later! Without question, Paul was operating on a different level of ministry than most men. Yet he, like the great men and women before him, recognized that God blessed him so that he could be a blessing. He told the churches at Ephesus and Corinth:

> *Surely you have heard about the administration of God's grace that was given to me for you.*
> —EPHESIANS 3:2, EMPHASIS ADDED

> *I may seem to be boasting too much about the authority given to us by the Lord. But our authority builds you up; it doesn't tear you down.*
> —2 CORINTHIANS 10:8, NLT, EMPHASIS ADDED

So God gave Paul a powerful portion of His grace to help, not hurt, other people. There were needs in the people, and Paul was the "pipe" through which God flowed to meet those needs. Let me say it another way. If the people didn't need building up, there would have been no reason for God to pour out so much grace on Paul. Every next-level blessing we experience has far-reaching purpose in the lives of others, and not an ounce of it is wasted.

Every next-level blessing you experience
has far-reaching purpose in the lives of
others, and not an ounce of it is wasted.

WHO WILL BENEFIT FROM YOUR NEXT LEVEL?

It seems to me that if God elevates people to the next level so they can be a blessing to others, then the key to entering the next level is having others on our mind. Stop and ask yourself, "How will someone else be blessed if God blesses me?" If you only have yourself on your mind, you are not prepared or in position for God to flow through you and bless others.

It's really all about motives. Think about it. *Why* do you want a promotion at work? *Why* do you want a newer car or a bigger house? *Why* do you want that relationship? *Why* do you want to write that book? *Why* do you want to put your ministry on television? It's all about motives. Motives are the why behind what you do. They reveal what is truly in your heart and are one of God's litmus tests to determine if you are ready for the next level.

It's not that we can't have personal goals and desires. However, God seems to get most involved when His grace can be leveraged to benefit the lives of others. This means that when He bestows blessings, He looks for the initial beneficiary of His blessing to take what He's given and use a portion of it to bless others.

The life of Abraham serves as an example of this principle. God told him that He was going to bless him so that he could be a blessing to others. (See Genesis 12:2–3.) Abraham became a tool to pass on a covenant relationship from one generation to the next. Even today, thousands of years later, people from every kindred and tongue are benefiting from the covenant

135

God made with this one man. Think about it. God blessed *one man* thousands of years ago so that today you and I would also be blessed. That's exceedingly, abundantly above what Abraham could have imagined. The question is, who will benefit from your next-level blessing?

Next-Level Concepts

The key to entering the next level is having others on your mind. God seems to get most involved when His grace can be leveraged to benefit the lives of others.

TAKE THE FAST LANE

Reaching the next level never happens overnight. However, there are some roads that seem to get you there faster than others. Living a life of giving is clearly one of them. I like to equate it to living life in the "HOV lane." HOV stands for "high-occupancy vehicle." The HOV lane is a part of the highway dedicated to drivers who carry more than one passenger. It's designed to encourage carpooling and get commuters to their destination faster than if they drove alone. Hence, the traffic using the HOV lane might be moving at 40 mph while single-occupant lanes are crawling at 10 mph. Both lanes will eventually get you to your destination. However, the pace and comfort of the journey can vary dramatically between the two.

So why don't more drivers choose the HOV lane during rush hour? There are a number of reasons. To begin with, it's not legal for everyone. Only drivers with two or more passengers can use these lanes during peak hours. It seems you have to be willing to help someone else get to their destination in order to receive the benefit of using the HOV lane. Sound familiar?

Another reason drivers don't choose the HOV lane is that carpooling can be inconvenient. After you have put in a full day's work, you just want to go home. No one wants to wait around for others to finish work. Likewise, no one wants to make an extra trip to drop off someone before they can go home. It's inconvenient. Yet the inconvenience of helping someone else get to their destination is miniscule compared to the agony of sitting in a lane of traffic that's going nowhere while other cars are zipping down the HOV lane.

Next-Level Concepts

New levels come to those who are willing to help others reach theirs. Clearly, living a life of giving puts you in the fast lane toward your next level.

This is why Jesus says, "Give, and it will be given to you" (Luke 6:38, NKJV). In other words, if you want "it" given, you must first be willing to give it. Another verse says:

The generous will prosper; those who refresh others will themselves be refreshed.
—PROVERBS 11:25, NLT

If you read the same verse as a question and answer, its meaning becomes even clearer.

- **Question**: How can you receive refreshment?

- **Answer**: Be willing to refresh someone else.

Again, it sounds like new levels come to those who are willing to help others reach theirs. So if you want a new level, ask yourself this question: *How am I using my current level to help others?* For instance, if you want a new level of financial prosperity, how are you using what you currently have to help someone else? If you want your skill or talent to be recognized on a larger scale, how are you presently using your talents to enrich the lives of others?

As I was writing this chapter, I came across an article in *USA Today* that I believe demonstrates what I've shared thus far. It is entitled "Good Deeds in Bad Times" and describes the generosity of some people during the 2008–09 recession. The article shares how some business owners gave to others in order to be a blessing. For example, in Montana, a florist gave away free bouquets each week to encourage people who needed encouragement. In Alabama, the owner of a pharmacy gave each of his full-time employees $700 with the stipulation that they had to give 15 percent to charity. And in Santa Cruz, California, a number of local businesses chipped in to help young women who couldn't afford prom dresses. Moreover, some local hairstyling shops offered their services, and dry cleaners offered free dry cleaning.[24]

Little did these businesses know that as they gave, they were setting themselves up to receive. Their actions set a law in motion—the law of sowing and reaping. As they refreshed others, they themselves will be refreshed. As they have given, it will be given back to them—good measure, pressed down, shaken together, and running over. It's a law that cannot be changed or denied—a law that, if engaged, puts you in the fast lane to the next level.

Next-Level Concepts

How can you receive refreshment? Be willing to refresh someone else. If you want to go to a new level, ask yourself, *How am I using my current level to help others?*

GIVING TO GOD PRODUCES EXPONENTIAL EFFECTS

If giving to others enables us to take the "HOV lane" to our next level, then giving to God is like taking the autobahn. When you give your time, talent, and treasure to God, you get biblical-sized results. Going back to my earlier example of the time my wife and I gave to a family in need, we didn't give just because there was a need. We meet people every day with needs. We gave because we believed we were giving to God. We were giving to what we call a "God project."

Now, this may sound a little strange. You may be thinking, "What is a 'God project'? If He's God, why can't He finance His own project? And how do you know it's God asking you to give and not just your emotions?" These are all legitimate questions. Let me answer them.

To begin with, a God project is any good work that God asks you to support in order to get His will done. A dear friend of mine who leads an international medical foundation describes it as a calling. He said that for years he looked at the television images of starving and sickly children in Africa and was unfazed. However, once he was given the opportunity to see firsthand the ravaging effects of war, famine, and sickness on people, he could no longer turn away. God was now asking him to get involved. No one was asking for donations. The only thing he saw was a need that his heart could no longer ignore. What a great definition for a God project! It's something God shows you that your heart can't turn away from or ignore.

Next-Level Concepts

A God project is any good work He asks
you to support in order to get His will
done. It's something He shows you that your
heart can't turn away from or ignore.

So why doesn't God just deal with tragedies like these Himself? Why does He want us to support the need? The reason is that when God created the earth, He gave it to man. Psalm 115:16 says, "The highest heavens belong to the Lord, but the earth he has given to man." Therefore, men and women are the only species with legal authority to rule the earth. God makes this principle exceedingly clear in the very first chapter of Scripture:

> *Then God said, "Let us make man in our image, in our likeness, and let them rule over the fish of the sea and the birds of the air, over the livestock, over all the earth, and over all the creatures that move along the ground."*
> —Genesis 1:26

Human beings are the only part of creation authorized to operate and control the earth. Animals do not have this authority, and neither do angels. Even God Himself has chosen to submit Himself to His Word and work through people. He gave the earth to man. Therefore, when God wants to legally and effectively get His will done on earth, He looks for a man or woman to partner with Him to do it. This is why Jesus, the Son of God, had to humble Himself and become a man of flesh and blood. He legally defeated the enemy as the Son of Man and regained dominion over the earth. Through our faith in Him, He has given that dominion back to us.

Could God come down and feed the children in Africa?

Yes. Could He stop every person who attempts to commit a crime? Yes. However, He has given that responsibility to us. It's our earth. If there is a need God wants to meet, He looks for someone on earth who will partner with Him to meet it.

Next-Level Concepts

When God wants to legally and effectively get His will done on earth, He looks for a man or woman to partner with Him to do it.

Now, here's the really cool part. If God needs something done on the earth, He looks to us. However, because we need the ability and wisdom to do it, we look to Him. This means you and I can access His strength and His resources.

Let me put it another way. Each time you participate in a God project, you get equipped with His provision of grace to get the job done. This is why my wife and I constantly stay prayerful about giving. Every time we choose to give to God's projects, He elevates us on His "go-to" list and equips us with an abundant supply of resources so that we can do even greater things for Him in the future. The Bible confirms this, declaring:

> *God can bless you with everything you need, and you will always have more than enough to do all kinds of good things for others.*
> —2 CORINTHIANS 9:8, CEV

My friend, God will bless you with everything you need so that you can abound in His good works. The way to keep His blessings coming is to keep the good works flowing. And through it all, He will receive praise and glory.

Remember, next-level blessings are never just for you.

God's eternal eyes are looking at countless lives around you and coming after you. He is weaving an immeasurable tapestry of love and grace, and *you* get to be a part of it! Be open to what He is doing. Prepare yourself for the new things ahead. Maintain a teachable spirit with those who are mentoring you. And receive the power of His grace daily. As you look for opportunities to be a blessing to others, your next level of blessing will come looking for you! It's only a matter of time.

Next-Level Concepts

As you look for opportunities to be a blessing to others, your next level of blessing will come looking for you! It's only a matter of time.

If you have a "Better Than Ever" story you'd like to share, submit it to us at www.nextlevel-living.com.

NEXT-LEVEL ACTION STEPS

1. When was the last time you were inspired to help someone else? Describe the situation. What was the result in the other person's life? How about your own life?

_____

_____

_____

_____

_____

2. Look over your income from the previous year and estimate how much you spent in the categories below. Does the data reflect a heart that desires to help others?

Category	Amount Spent	What does this say to you? What changes should you make?
Entertainment		
Vacations		
Charity		

3. Can you think of a time when someone you know experienced a next-level blessing and they shared it with you? If so, describe what happened and tell how it affected you.

_____

_____

_____

_____

_____

4. Is there someone you know right now who has a need or dream you can help fulfill? Do they need money, material goods, a connection with someone you know, or just some time and attention? Who is it, and what are you going to do to help them?

_____

_____

_____

_____

_____

Activity for Advancement: If you were given $100,000, how would you spend it? List each item you would purchase or service you would pay for in order of priority. Give an approximate dollar value for each until it totals $100,000. Does your answer reflect being "others minded"? What changes might you need to make in your thinking?

_____

_____

_____

_____

_____

Scriptures for Meditation: Proverbs 3:27–28; Matthew 25:35–40; Galatians 6:10; Hebrews 13:16

NOTES

1. NBA.com: Rajon Rondo Player Info, http://www.nba.com/home/playerfile/rajon_rondo/career_stats.html.

2. Howard Schultz and Dori Jones Yang, Pour Your Heart Into It: How Starbucks Built a Company One Cup at a Time (New York: Hyperion, 1997), 23.

3. See Spencer Johnson, Who Moved My Cheese? An Amazing Way to Deal With Change in Your Work and in Your Life (New York: G. P. Putnam's Sons, 1998).

4. Steve Jobs, 2005 Stanford Commencement Address, accessed at Stanford University News, "'You've Got to Find What You Love,' Jobs Says," June 14, 2005, http://news.stanford.edu/news/2005/june15/jobs-061505.html.

5. American Congregations at the Beginning of the 21st Century, National Congregations Study, available at http://www.soc.duke.edu/natcong/Docs/NCSII_report_final.pdf.

6. Yogesh Ambekar, "Michael Phelps: Biography of World's Best Swimmer," http://www.buzzle.com/editorials/8-27-2004-58516.asp

7. Ian Spiegelman, "Michael Phelps' Freakish Physique Explained," August 17, 2008, http://gawker.com/5038018/michael-phelps-freakish-physique-explained, http://www.baltimoresun.com/sports/olympics/bal-sp.phelps09mar09,0,7665681.story

8. Ibid.

9. Steve Mazzucchi, "Go For Gold! Learn to Train Like an Olympian," August 7, 2008, http://www.msnbc.msn.com/id/25847528/ns/health-fitness/t/go-gold-learn-train-olympian

10. Kevin Joy, "A Voice from the Streets has the Sound of a Fairy Tale," The Columbus Dispatch, January 4, 2011, http://www.dispatch.com/live/content/local_news/stories/2011/01/04/voice-from-streets-has-sound-of-fairy-tale.html

11. Marcus Buckingham and Donald O. Clifton, Now, Discover Your Strengths (New York: The Free Press, 2001), 21–22.

12. Brandon Guarneri, "Kobe Bryant: He Trains Harder and Longer Than Anyone Else in the NBA," Men's Fitness, http://www.mensfitness.com/lifestyle/interview/kobe-bryant.

13. TigerWoods.com, "Tiger's Daily Routine," available at http://www.tigerwoods.com/fitness/tigerDailyRoutine.

14. Ed Cole Library, "Coleisms," http://edcole.org/index.php?fuseaction=coleisms.showColeism&id=94&keywords=practice&page=

15. Amber Riviere, http://www.rockyourgenius.com/about/

16. Geoffrey Colvin, "What it Takes to be Great," Fortune Magazine, October 19, 2006, http://money.cnn.com/magazines/fortune/fortune_archive/2006/10/30/8391794/index.htm.

17. Geoff Colvin, Talent Is Overrated: What Really Separates World-Class Performers From Everybody Else (New York: Portfolio, 2008), 36–38.

18. WENN.com, "Hudson Makes History With 'Vogue' Cover," accessed September 11, 2007, link no longer available.

19. Los Angeles Times, "Steelers' Mike Tomlin Credit Mentors for his Quick Ascent," January 27, 2009, http://articles.latimes.com/2009/jan/27/sports/sp-nflrep27

20. http://www.searchquotes.com/quotation/All_coaching_is,_is_taking_a_player _where_he_can't_take_himself./160034/

21. Lois J. Zachary, The Mentor's Guide: Facilitating Effective Learning Relationships (San Francisco: Jossey-Bass, 2000), xiii.

22. David Foster with Pablo F. Fenjves, Hitman: Forty Years Making Music, Topping Charts and Winning Grammys (New York: Pocket Books, 2008), 73.

23. Ibid., 75.

24. Judy Keen, "Good Deeds in Bad Times: Financial Woes Spur Kind Acts," USA Today, March 31, 2001, http://www.usatoday.com/printedition/news/20090310/1agooddeeds11_st.art.htm.

ABOUT THE AUTHOR

D ION WOODS IS a transformational speaker who is passionate about helping people achieve new levels of living through the application of biblical truth. Armed with more than a decade of service to corporations, churches, and individuals around the country, his desire is to see people reach their full potential in God. Dion and his wife, Belinda, have two wonderful children and live in Virginia.

.

CONTACT THE AUTHOR

NEXT LEVEL MANAGEMENT: 888-892-6449

WWW.NEXTLEVEL-LIVING.COM

www.ingramcontent.com/pod-product-compliance
Lightning Source LLC
LaVergne TN
LVHW051103080426
835508LV00019B/2035

Interview
For
Marriage

A Biblical Perspective on Dating

☙☙

Dr. Ryan Jouett